My Grandfather's Watch:
Family and Faith Across Generations

My Grandfather's Watch:
Family and Faith Across Generations

John David Connolly

Maggie Rose Connolly, Editor

A self-published work
2020

Unless otherwise stated, all biblical references are quoted from the New Revised Standard Version (NRSV) (Division of Christian Education of the National Council of the Churches of Christ in the United States of America, 1989)

The views and opinions expressed in this book belong solely to the author and in no way represent the views of the US Navy, the US Navy Chaplain Corps, or the Evangelical Lutheran Church in America.

First Printing: 2020

Paperback ISBN 978-1-7348393-1-9

eBook ISBN 978-1-7348393-0-2

Published by John David Connolly

My Grandfather's Watch:
Family and Faith Across Generations

John David Connolly

Maggie Rose Connolly, Editor

A self-published work
2020

First Printing: 2020

Paperback ISBN 978-1-7348393-1-9

eBook ISBN 978-1-7348393-0-2

Published by John David Connolly

Dedication

Over the years, I have often wondered where I came from to help me become who I am today. There is absolutely no doubt that our personalities are a composite of our ancestry and our experiences in life. Experiences are something that you go through personally and have an idea of why they affect you the way they do. Your ancestry, on the other hand, is an entirely different matter. Your parents, grandparents, aunts, uncles, cousins, etc. are all an integral part of your DNA. You can neither choose it nor abandon it; your family is part of who you are more permanently than any tattoo will ever be.

My family was chosen for me from before time by our gracious and loving God, and God chose them perfectly for me. And no matter how dysfunctional we may ever seem, God also chose us for those who come after us.

This compilation of the crazy and loving things that your ancestors did will help you understand a little better who you are, and that your nutty ways are nothing compared to what you came from. Maggie, my beautiful daughter, I love you dearly, and these are the stories of your life; they are dedicated entirely to you.

Contents

Introduction

Train up a child in the way he should go, and when he is old, he will not depart
from it.

Proverbs 22:6

I have in my possession at least two watches that belonged to some of my grandfathers. I have found that it is quite common that a young man will receive his grandfather's watch as something to remember his grandfather by. More often than not, that watch will become one of the young man's most prized possessions. This is certainly the case with me and the watches that I have been given, which belonged to my grandfathers. The watches themselves keep time very poorly and I never wear them, but yet I cherish them. They mean the world to me because they remind me of my grandfathers and all that these wonderful men meant to me.

Yet, it bears asking – was a watch all that I inherited from them? Obviously not. Grandfathers, it seems, pass on much more to their grandchildren than simple trinkets. They pass on years of wisdom. They pass on visions of the past and future. They pass on values and principles. They pass on the guidelines that we, in turn, will pass on to our children and grandchildren. They also pass on habits, good ones and bad. Obviously, this does not just apply to grandfathers, but grandmothers too.

Please, take a moment and remember the times spent with grandparents. Usually, they are far enough removed from you that their guidance does not seem like meddling or micro-managing your life. Yet they are close enough that even the most intimate conversations and guidance are not out of bounds.

Over the years my grandparents spent a tremendous amount of time molding and shaping me, directly and indirectly. No matter where I was or what I was doing, as a group, they took great interest in me and my sister and our brother personally. Asking any of my cousins you will find the same from them. Each grandparent was quite different, with different interests and focus on life. Where one would monitor my life spiritually another would monitor it educationally. Thinking back now, it is almost overwhelming to consider the way that God wrapped love around me so completely with my grand-parents.

After high school, I enlisted in the Navy for six years. Sometimes I spent a year or more without seeing some of my grandparents. Often I was terrible about writing to them or keeping in contact with them. However, never did their love or care for me waiver. One grandmother, in particular, would send me, on a regular basis, a box of cookies to share. Inevitably in that box of cookies was a scripture passage or meditation that she had placed in with the cookies that connected with me in exactly the way that I needed at that point in my life.

One thing that you do in the Navy is to stand a lot of watches. Whenever you are on watch you are in part responsible for the safety and security of your ship and shipmates during your watch. For people like the captain of a ship, his or her entire tenure in the Navy is their watch, and a good captain takes it very seriously. Often you will hear a person like that comment on a particular subject like drugs in the Navy as, "Not on my watch." Here they are implying that their watch never ends, and this atrocity will not occur while they are in the Navy.

Grandparents approach their grandchildren in much the same way. From the time you are born your grandparents are "on watch" for you, for them, and for their family. They guard you against danger and impart to you their wisdom and guidance. You can rest assured that my grandparents were "on watch" for me, and I thank God for the blessing this has been for me.

Sure my grandfather's watch was made of gold and jewels, but it was also heart and soul. The grandparents that had a part in raising me all took this responsibility very seriously and without them, I would not be the person I am today. As each grandparent would take their turn "on watch" they would share that moment with me completely. They took this time to show me how to paint, how to bail hay, how to replace a spark plug, how QSL cards work, and most of all, how Jesus loves me. They would share the Gospel with me directly, but they also shared it with me in the way they lived and in what they valued.

The stories that I share here are just a small taste of how my grandparents shaped and influenced my life. Early in my life, they cared for me. They fed me, cleaned me up, changed my diaper, and told me stories. As I got older, I was able to take care of myself, and in most cases, they were still able to care for themselves. We began to have adventures together. The times we were able to be together were magical. As they each approached their twilight years, our roles began to reverse. I, along with the rest of my family, became the caretakers, and they became the mischievous children. However, none of them lost their focus on the goal of being with Jesus. Even when their eyes became cloudy, and so did their minds, they perked up for a good Gospel song or a verse of scripture. They showed me how to live and they showed me how to die.

They each stood the watch themselves over me for many years. I, in turn, stood the watch over them. This was not an obligation or a chore; this was a privilege. Each of my grandparents has now joined the church triumphant, and I still stand the watch in their honor as I look forward to continuing the watch with my daughter and eventual grandchildren.

A Grandfather's Blessing

When Israel saw Joseph's sons, he said, "Who are these?" Joseph said to his father, "They are my sons, whom God has given me here." And he said, "Bring them to me, please, that I my bless them." Now the eyes of Israel were dim with age, and he could not see well. So Joseph brought them near him; and he kissed them and embraced them. Israel said to Joseph, "I did not expect to see your face; and here God has let me see your children also."

Genesis 48:8-11

A grandparent's blessing is a particularly special thing. It is a rare event that a grandparent will bless their grandchildren in such a dramatic and sensational way, but it can and does happen. From this account, Israel (Jacob) went on to bless the twelve tribes of Israel, his twelve sons, with a very specific blessing for each of them, but he started his series of blessings with a couple of his grandchildren.

The blessings that our grandparents pass on to us come in so many different ways, but the most common is the kiss and the embrace that Jacob used. Never would I visit any of my grandparents, regardless of my age, when a kiss and a hug was not part of the visit. The love that is shared between grandparents and their grandchildren is immeasurable, much like the descendants of Jacob. Whenever I would show up at one of my grandparents' homes, it was as if I had not been seen in years, even if I had just been there yesterday or a few hours ago.

Although I grew up with a distorted understanding of normal family life because of my parents' divorce, I was doubly blessed because of the new grandparents that my parents' subsequent marriages brought to me. Grandma and Grandpa were my stepfather's parents and were unique beyond words. They lived in Gaston County North Carolina but were from upstate New York. Grandma had grown up in Alabama and found her way in her early years to Ithaca, NY where Grandpa lived. She was a Southerner, transplanted to the North, and then returned to the South later in life. Each step of the way they picked up and embraced different elements of the culture, which she lovingly shared with my sister, brother, and me.

Grandma was a cook par excellence, and with the adage to never trust a skinny cook; you could trust Grandma. Although she could, and often did, prepare the typical southern fare, normally she would stretch her creative wings and soar to areas we had never heard of. She often enjoyed delving into various ethnic and cultural dishes that were out there and made them to perfection. She introduced me to various German dishes, Mexican dishes, Chinese dishes, and so many others that I could not possibly remember them all. The truly amazing thing about the variety we enjoyed at her table was the fact that most of what we enjoyed came from her own garden.

If Grandma was a cook par excellence, then Grandpa was a gardener par excellence. Vegetables that no one else in that small North Carolina town would even try to tackle – Grandpa grew. He grew the normal tomatoes and green beans (in biblical proportions), but he also grew eggplant, rhubarb, dill, chives, peppers of a rainbow of colors and types, squashes, and various berries. Even in the squashes, he would seek to find varieties that were unusual, and always grew them well.

Between them, they stretched our culinary palates in ways that we had never before dreamed. A meal with them was always an event to behold, and a new and pleasant gastronomic experience. But, as much of a blessing as their culinary skills and gifts were, the greater gift was the time spent with them.

Following my parents' divorce, all relations around me seemed to be strained and difficult. An uncertainty overshadowed relationships with other people to such a point that I was unclear of my standing with them, and it was often incumbent upon them to help define my relationship with them. At five and six years of age I did not understand this, nor did I have the faculties to reach out myself to others to define that relationship. Fortunately, adults in my life like Grandma and Grandpa were willing and able to do that for me.

From the very beginning, they both took me in as their own and looked upon me as their grandson although there was no blood connection. As with Jacob and his grandchildren, I could always count on a hug and a kiss from Grandma. She was genuinely interested in my wellbeing, and what was going on in my life. Grandpa also welcomed me with open and loving arms, and always took the time to invite me into his world of hobbies, gardening, and technical projects.

One of Grandma's greatest blessings to me was her straightforward discussion and confirmation of my relationship with my stepfather. She recognized a confusion and apprehension on my part and affirmed to me not only her love for me but also his. "You know, Jonny really loves you, and does his very best to take care of you kids." It was very affirming to not only understand this implicitly but to also hear it and receive it from another source explicitly.

Blessings are a two-way street and should go both directions. They also come in a variety of forms. When Papaw was turning eighty I really wanted to make him feel very special. He and I had shared a number of things over the years in our fondness for each other, and I began to ramble through my memories of what would express my love for him. I thought about baseball and for him, of course, the Braves, but we already went to see them every year. I thought about the way that he and I would go enjoy a cup of apple cider together on Mr. Jim's front porch, but unfortunately, Mr. Jim had died several years previous. I then stumbled upon the perfect solution – gospel music.

He and I went to churches and other venues all over that area of North Carolina together in order to enjoy gospel music together; or as he would put it, to go to a "Sangin'". I discussed this with Mamaw and some others in my family and we all agreed that having a birthday party including a gospel quartet was the way to go. Mamaw knew of a local group and gave them a call to see if they were willing to come. Fortunately, they knew Phil (Papaw) and were delighted to come to sing for us, but especially for him.

On the day of the party, we held it at the fellowship hall of the Methodist Church and invited the community of friends and family to join us for the celebration. The fellowship hall was decorated, food was spread that would feed the entire county, and friends far and wide gathered for the celebration. Papaw sat there and simply relished the idea of a quartet coming to sing for him for his birthday.

Towards the end of the party, Papaw came over to me and shared perhaps his most tender moment ever with me. He reached across the folding table where we had been eating and grasped my hand in his leathery grasp. He then said, "John David, they tell me this was your idea."

"Yes, sir."

With almost a tear in his eye, he said to me, "Boy, this means the world to me; I can't believe you did all this for me. Thank you." He held my hand for a moment longer then returned to enjoy the rest of the "Sangin'".

I am not sure who walked away that day the more blessed, Papaw or me. I think we will call it a draw and be OK with it. Perhaps that is the way that blessings are supposed to work. It really was a great day.

Coffee Cake

A capable wife who can find? She is far more precious than jewels. The heart of her
husband trusts in her, and he will have no lack of gain. She does him good, and
not harm, all the days of her life. She seeks wool and flax, and works with
willing hands. She is like the ships of the merchant, she brings her food from
far away. She rises while it is still night and provides food for her household
and tasks for her servant-girls.

Proverbs 31:10-15

Mawmaw and Pawpaw were my great-grandparents. They
married in 1913 and had a love that was more intense than you could
possibly imagine. They absolutely adored each other well into sixty
plus years of marriage. Until the day they each died, they longed to
be by each other's side and enjoy what life offered, together. After
my grandfather died my grandmother still enjoyed life, but it just
wasn't the same experience without her lifelong friend, soul mate, and
companion.

Both of them loved and lived life to its fullest extent and did their
best to experience all that God provided for them. Pawpaw became
an accomplished engineer, and, as such, was a tremendous influence
in my life. Mawmaw was quite accomplished musically and in the
culinary arts. They also did quite well financially, especially after
Pawpaw opened his own heating and air conditioning consulting firm.
But, they definitely did not start financially well off or accomplished
in their respective interests.

Growing up, for the most part in the late 1800's, Mawmaw did
not really need to learn many of the more domestic characteristics
normally associated with wives. Her mother provided for her
everything that she needed, and, unfortunately for my grandmother,
her mother did not include her so that she could learn some of the
basics around the kitchen. However, after she and my grandfather
were married she wanted desperately to care for him as was typical of
that time.

Mawmaw knew fairly well how to boil water, and could even
hard boil an egg – very hard boiled. She had seen coffee made
before, and had once even seen a cake made; she had just never made

one herself. She more or less knew how to use the basic components of the kitchen and how to build the fire for the stove (it is worth remembering at this point in our country's history that electrical appliances were few and far between). With this "wealth" of knowledge, my grandmother felt sufficiently armed to attempt a coffee cake for her new husband. Although she had never had coffee cake herself, she knew that her new husband really enjoyed it, and was actually one of his favorites.

Although her mother had never really shown her how to follow a recipe, she had loaded Mawmaw up with an armload of them when she and my grandfather got married. Mawmaw searched through the stack of recipes to find one for coffee cake, and found just the right one. Promptly, she began to gather her ingredients, not really certain what each of them did, but she diligently went about the task of finding each item and carefully measuring them to the desired quantities. She was determined that her new husband was going to love this cake.

Mawmaw carefully read the recipe and found that she had just enough time to prepare the cake for Pawpaw before he returned home so that just as he walked in she would be able to present him with this wonderful cake. She set about combining the ingredients just as the recipe called out. She sifted the flour to get out undesired lumps and "bits". She combined her liquid ingredients, and then spent another twenty minutes getting the eggshells back out of the mixture.

Each item in the ingredients list was called out in the recipe one by one and she combined them in just as the recipe called for them, until the last ingredient. She read through the recipe once again, but just couldn't find where this one ingredient was mixed in. Finally giving in, and just letting common sense take over, she combined it in with the other ingredients just as each previous ingredient had been.

Cooking in a wood burning stove is somewhat of a trick. In modern times we simply adjust the controls to the desired temperature, set a digital timer for optimum accuracy, and go watch TV until it is time to remove the cake. In the early years of the 20th century this just was not the case. A wood burning stove did have a thermometer, but to "adjust" the temperature required much more work. If you want to raise the temperature you must add more wood or open the vents to allow in more air. Lowering the temperature you had to close the vents to the fire and/or wait for some of the wood to burn down. In either case, you had to make an adjustment then wait to see if you had the desired effect, which could take quite some time. Then the challenge was to keep it at that temperature. The other amusing aspect to these stoves was the fact that your thermometer may read the temperature perfectly, but only in one spot. To believe that your stove was uniformly heated was simply a dream. Having a temperature differential of 30° across your oven was common, and this is where knowing your oven became paramount

Mawmaw did her best to get the oven to 375°, and was able to get it there and hold it there much easier than she had suspected that it would be. She quickly placed the first masterpiece of her young marriage into the oven and sat back to enjoy the fruits of her labor. After about 20 minutes she noticed that the temperature had dropped to 350° and quickly piled more wood into the firebox. By the time the temperature finally leveled off it was about 410° and eventually returned to about 375° at about the time the cake was to come out of the oven.

Just as Mawmaw was pulling her "cake" from the oven, Pawpaw was coming in the front door looking for his new bride. When she pulled it out, only one side was really smoking, the other side looked just about right. Mawmaw began to cry, she was certain that her new husband would run off and find a wife that knew how to cook. She was distraught over her lack of knowledge and her failure to ensure that she was better prepared for this day before she was married. With tears streaming down her face, Mawmaw presented the half lump of smoldering coal to her husband, uttering something completely unintelligible about her failure.

Pawpaw was a gracious man. Actually, he was probably one of the most gracious, loving, and forgiving people who ever existed. He calmly accepted the chunk of coal, and thanked her while lovingly kissing her cheek and wiping some of the flour from her forehead. He set the cake on the counter and found a knife to cut it with, then carefully cut a piece from the less charred side of the cake. To his surprise, despite the unseemly looks of the opposite side, this side looked quite good. He was already thinking that he had found a diamond in this lump of coal. Mawmaw provided him with a cup of coffee since she had mastered the percolator last week.

Pawpaw sat down at the table, prepared to fully enjoy his cake and coffee, and besides that it was coffee cake, which was one of his favorites. He had a sip of coffee and was pleased that his new bride had finally mastered the percolator. He raised his fork to take a bite of the coffee cake and cut it with the edge of the fork finding it surprisingly moist for as burned as the other side was. He scooped the tender piece of cake onto his fork and hoisted it to his mouth with divided anticipation. At first, he found it to be moist and tasty, and then another flavor began to creep in. It wasn't completely unpleasant, but it was very unexpected. He finished chewing the piece and carefully swallowed it.

As mentioned previously, Pawpaw was nothing if he wasn't gracious. He loved my grandmother with all his heart, and odd flavor or not, he was going to finish that piece of cake. As he deliberately cut each piece he complimented my grandmother on her new found culinary skill, although they both agreed that gently turning the cake may prevent future uneven cooking. Pawpaw asked her, "Bert, this is awful good, what did you put in it?" (Although her name was Winnie, he always called her Bert. I never quite understood this, but I found it to be a loving part of their unique love language with each other.).

Mawmaw responded by recounting the steps she went through, reading off the list of ingredients to him, "2 cups of flour, 2 eggs, 1 cup of milk, a teaspoon of baking powder, a half teaspoon of salt, a half cup of sugar, 4 tablespoons of butter, and a cup of coffee."

"A cup of coffee?" my grandfather quizzed incredulously.

"Yep, that kind of got me too." Mawmaw said. "Every other ingredient it told me what to do with it, but the cup of coffee it just left out there. I figured they had forgotten to describe how to put it in, so I just put in a cup of grounds at the end and mixed it up the way I had every other ingredient. I probably should have put it in with the rest of the dry ingredients, but it was too late at that point. Do you think that made a difference?"

"No," Pawpaw replied, "I believe that you could have put it in at just about any time and it would have the same effect." Then he sat there and finished his piece of coffee cake, smiling with each and every bite.

It was actually some time later that Pawpaw finally worked up the courage to discuss Mawmaw's culinary skills with her, but it was with his usual grace and love. Eventually, they both laughed over it, and learned from it. The mistake that she feared would destroy their marriage actually acted to strengthen it, and years later when she shared this story with me it was to highlight to me how much they loved each other and how much she had to learn in the kitchen when they first got married.

Their marriage and their care for one another has been an inspiration to me and many others in our own relationships. I just pray that my wife and I will be able to find that kind of compassion for each other throughout our marriage as well, and still laugh about the things when we first got married like they did.

Moving the Outhouse

Pretty much anyone that has ever had to accomplish a difficult goal has run into roadblocks of one form or another. They seem to be as much a part of life as the goal we are seeking to accomplish is. However, these unfortunate roadblocks are rarely expected, and cause us to react in a way that is equally unexpected. Think, for instance, of the last time you were hammering and missed the nail but hit your thumb instead. For many people at that moment their vocabulary seems to take on an entirely different tone; a tone that is not generally acceptable in Sunday school.

Now, although my grandfather's language is not something of family lore, the events surrounding him are. At the same time, many of those events would lead the average person to use what one of my seminary professors referred to as, "football words." Those are the words that many men feel are very appropriate while watching a football game that make the children go to Mom later for a vocabulary lesson. This, of course, causes Mom to have a discussion with Dad about words he will not be using around the children.

If ever there was an event that would cause my grandfather to use, "football words," and feel the remorse that Isaiah did, the tale told here would be that event. Chances are everyone involved was using multiple variations on those words as this entire event played out, but those have been lost forever.

There are certain things from life of years gone by, which seem completely foreign to us today. Some come from technological advances, shifting sense of values, outside forces on our society or others. The basic needs and necessities in life, however, have not changed since the dawn of civilization. One of these is the basic need for toilet facilities of one form or another.

In the days before modern indoor plumbing toilet facilities were maintained outside of the home, and usually some distance from it.

The maintenance of these facilities was straightforward, unpleasant, but quite required, and a family could not afford to be without their requisite outhouse. When establishing a home this either meant that the family had to build a new outhouse or put up an existing one. This is exactly the circumstance my family found themselves in when they bought the farmhouse that I came to know and love.

In 1950 my grandmother, Mamaw, worked for the US Census as a field worker, and went from home to home to confirm the census numbers of the homes that she was assigned. One of her assigned homes was an old farmhouse, out a dead-end road, in the outer portions or Iredell County. During the course of this assignment she discovered that the farmhouse was for sale, and met much of what she and my grandfather, Papaw, were looking for in a farm.

The farm was about 130 acres of rolling meadow land with a small stream running through the center of it. On it was a large, wood frame farmhouse that would just fit their growing family. In it had running water to the kitchen, if you used the hand pump correctly, but had yet to build indoor plumbing facilities for the restroom. Until that time, my grandparents would need to have their family use an outhouse. As luck would have it, the home they were presently in had an outhouse that they could take with them on their move to their new farmhouse. They made an offer on the farm, appropriate arrangements for financing, and moved their family to their new farm.

Moving in those days was no small feat. Usually, it meant gathering any family and friends with trucks and tractors that you could find, strapping your earthly belongings to various vehicles, and making a grand caravan of ragtag vehicles across whatever distance divided you from your new home. This, of course, was no different for my grandparents and their family than it was for any other family of that time. Fortunately, however, for them was the fact that the move they were to make was less than ten miles.

Most of the move went quite smoothly, and without a hitch. The various family furniture, clothing, and family members all made the move within the first day or so. Moving the outhouse was not quite so simple.

To move the outhouse took a larger vehicle than most of their other family belongings; after all, they were moving a small building from one location to another. Papaw, a few family members, and some friends all gathered at their old house and loaded the old outhouse onto Papaw's flatbed trailer. You can just imagine the amusement of seeing a 5 foot by 5 foot building picked up from above an old cesspit by a group of men and loaded on a trailer. No matter how carefully you try to keep your outhouse, at the end of the day it is still an outhouse over an open hole full of less than pleasant smells. Eventually, however, this group of men got the old outhouse loaded on the trailer and strapped down.

The route from the old house to the new farmhouse was a series of back country roads, passing by other homes and businesses. As Papaw traveled his route to his new home, he felt a certain amount of rye amusement as he towed that old outhouse past a series of houses from some of the more well-to-do families of the area, who already had indoor plumbing. His amusement subsided significantly when he felt a sudden surge in his Allis Chalmers tractor.

He knew that tractor as well as he knew any piece of his machinery, and a surge on a flat road was not one of the things that he had come to expect of it. His worst suspicion was confirmed when he looked back and saw that the tongue of his trailer had broken, and his trailer, along with his outhouse, had taken up residence in the front yard of one of his new neighbors along the way.

Papaw stopped his tractor, got down and assessed the situation. Unfortunately, he did not have the necessary tools or supplies to repair the broken trailer, nor did he have any other means immediately available to get his outhouse to his new home. Suffering from a sense of shame from the amusement he felt only moments before, he now had to swallow a significant amount of pride and go knock on the front door of his neighbor to explain the unfortunate circumstance.

Can you just imagine that kind of conversation? In his most polite and ingratiating way, he informed his neighbor of the bad sense of timing and luck that had befallen him, "You know, a funny thing happened as we were towing our outhouse past your home. Boy, it sure is a nice outhouse, but I'll need to come back for it in a day or so when I get my trailer repaired." He requested that he be allowed to come back for his outhouse and trailer later with the proper tools and supplies. For some unknown and incomprehensible reason, his neighbor actually agreed.

According to Papaw's normal rate of getting things done, it was almost a week before he was finally able to get back over to his neighbor's house to retrieve his trailer and outhouse. And, to make matters worse, it was getting late in the day when he was finally able to go. Out of a sense of wisdom for some sense of safety, Papaw had Mamaw follow him in their Ford just to keep lights on him so that other traffic could see this side-show coming.

Papaw had not had sufficient time to get a new tongue made for his trailer, which, of course, would have been the wise course of action. Instead, he devised a plan to "repair" his old trailer tongue. He took with him a couple of pieces of wood, along with some bailing wire and an old logging chain. He wrapped the broken tongue like you would a broken leg, and effectively splinted it. He then attached the "repaired" trailer to the tow hitch of the tractor and prepared for the remainder of the trip to his new farmhouse with an extra layer of protection in a logging chain wrapped around the whole catastrophe.

Tractors never can build up a tremendous speed, and they usually top out at about twenty-five to thirty miles per hour. Papaw gave that old tractor all it had, trying to get back to his new farmhouse with at least a little bit of sunlight remaining, but that was obviously going to be impossible. He knew that it would be close and that was why he had Mamaw to follow him in their Ford.

Mamaw stayed back at a safe distance, just in case the "repair" job failed again, and kept the headlights on Papaw so that other motorists would be able to see him. Part of Papaw's repair job included an old logging chain. Unfortunately, he did not spend a lot of time trying to make it snug nor keep it far from the ground. As they began their journey, the old logging chain began to drag on the road.

As dusk was beginning to fall, and the light was waning, the sparks created by that old logging chain on the road were spectacular. Papaw, of course, knew what was going on, and strategically chose to ignore it rather than lose any more daylight by stopping. Mamaw on the other hand, did not know what was going on, and panic overtook her.

From her perspective, she could see the old flatbed trailer being towed. Because of the outhouse on top of it, she had a difficult time even seeing that someone was driving the tractor which was towing the trailer. Add to that an immense shower of sparks which was emanating from the front end of that trailer and creating a massive rooster tail of sparks up and over the outhouse. Mamaw was absolutely convinced that the trailer had caught fire and their outhouse was going to burst into flames. On top of that was the concern that the tractor, along with Papaw, was in imminent danger of explosion or some other catastrophe.

Mamaw began to holler and honk her horn and cry and any number of other things to get Papaw's attention. Yet through it all, Papaw persisted, and stayed his course toward their new home. Papaw actually felt a certain amount of glee from the concern that Mamaw felt; of course, that subsided significantly later when Mamaw was able to fully express to him what she thought.

Eventually, Papaw, Mamaw, the trailer with the outhouse, and Papaw's rooster tail of sparks made it to their new farmhouse. It was sometime after dark before they ever pulled up, but now they were able to visit the facilities in privacy. But, there is more to that old outhouse than simply another building on the property.

You can imagine what it must have been like for a growing family to be moving into a new home and not have a place to do your business, privately. Granted, with Papaw and four boys they really weren't all that concerned, but Mamaw and one girl certainly were. None were happier than the ladies of the family when the new outhouse had been made fully ready for use; including toilet paper and a Sears & Roebuck catalog.

Mamaw was a real lady, but she was also a simple country lady. She had been born on a farm herself in a building without power, running water, or even a solid floor. This new home was the epitome of new and upcoming because it did have power, and a tin roof, and clapboard siding, and a real front porch. So, although the restroom facilities were exterior to the home, it was still the nicest house she had ever lived in, and it did not bother her at all that she had to walk outside in order to relieve herself. After all, you never know what you may see.

Not knowing what you may see or come across is exactly what did happen to Mamaw on one of her first visits to their new outhouse. As she emerged from their home to make her way across the yard to the outhouse she noted some movement in the grassy area near the outhouse, and she immediately froze. Not knowing what it might be, especially since it might not like you, you tend to tread lightly. So, being a little preemptively cautious, she stealthily reached down and found a relatively nice sized stone lying near her feet and carefully stood back up to her full height.

Mamaw was ready. She stood tall and proud ready to either fight or flee; of course if she did flee that did not resolve the reason she was out there to begin with so her preference was to fight, do her business, and then flee. She raised her throwing arm in preparation to shoo away whatever may be lurking near her outhouse so that she could proceed, and continued to creep ever closer to the outhouse and realize her eventual relief from an increasingly growing pressure inside her. Whatever was creeping near was not helping her bladder control concerns at all.

When she was still about 25 feet away, her stalker leapt up and, without thinking at all, Mamaw let fly her rock at her opponent. Simultaneously, she made a quick dash for the outhouse and relative safety and relief from building pressure. She was pretty confident that her rock had struck her opponent and that he had either been knocked out or scared away; either way was a win for her. A few minutes later she emerged from the outhouse, and the family dinner plans were no longer a significant concern; they were having rabbit for dinner. Mamaw had made a clean, powerful, square hit on a rabbit that she was convinced was a mountain lion about to pounce on her, but who was in no way going to prevent her from enjoying her moment of relief in her outhouse.

The lesson for you here is the family outhouse is precious, a thing of legend, and not something that you hinder anyone from being able to enjoy. It may not be pretty, but it is pretty important.

Spirits Are Ya There?

And after [Jesus] had dismissed the crowds, he went up the mountain by himself to pray. When evening came, he was there alone, but by this time the boat, battered by the waves, was far from the land, for the wind was against them. And early in the morning he came walking toward them on the sea. But when the disciples saw him walking on the sea, they were terrified, saying, "It is a ghost!" And they cried out in fear. But immediately Jesus spoke to them and said, "Take heart, it is I; do not be afraid."

Matthew 14:23-27

As humans, many things tend to startle and scare us. The unknown, the unexpected, the hard to accept or believe are all unsettling to us. We see something that should not normally be there and instinctively assume the supernatural, but then when we look we begin to realize that it is really what we expected after all.

In matters of faith many things appear supernatural to us, because we look upon what God is doing with human eyes and understanding. What is completely impossible for us is quite possible for God. All of this does not prevent us from being startled, but it does begin to explain why things of the spirit world do catch us off guard. As people of faith, however, we do not need to be afraid. We can "take heart" because our Lord comes to us in those moments we least expect it, in the way we need it the most.

Knowing our tendency to startle easily though is a great opportunity for us to have fun at each other's expense. We know by faith that God is much greater than any "spirit" we can conjure up, but we still tend to startle at the sight of such things.

Granny grew up in Texas, where the nights were hot and summer seemed to go on forever. The homes were your typical slat-board, whitewashed, wooden, A-frame homes. The foundations were normally rocks or bricks strategically piled at the load bearing points, but most of the crawlspace was open to the air. Most homes had a small sitting porch, which on some of those hot summer nights was the only cool spot. This particular night, that porch is where Granny and her friends were sitting, telling jokes and stories, and just enjoying each other's company.

Granny absolutely loved spending time with her friends. She did so in this early part of her life, and then at the end of her life they meant no less than they had earlier in her life. No matter what was going on, you could always count on the fact that Granny would surround herself with friends and family. On this hot summer night in Texas, Granny had just gotten back from a summer camp, and had missed her friends tremendously. So they had gathered on her front porch to catch up and enjoy the evening together.

At summer camp, kids learn all kinds of things. Some of them very practical and useful, some just fun, and some just don't seem to fit anywhere – but you learn them. That summer, some of Granny's friends at camp had taught her how to talk to the dead, or have a séance. Little by little Granny walked the group of them through the steps. Now, these friends of hers were simple country boys and girls, and not terribly sophisticated. However, this intrigued them to no end.

They knew all about plowing a field, tending to the herds, or harvesting the cotton, but they knew nothing of these fancy city terms, such as séances. However, if Granny said that it was fun then it must be! Who knows, maybe they'll get to talk to Uncle Gene who died last year when the mule kicked him.

Granny told them, "Now we all have to sit real close and quiet, and hold hands." So they all noisily scooted their ladder-back chairs closer to one another and held hands. Granny's tone went from a typically jovial to deadly serious. Her friends began to notice this, and the whites of their eyes became a little larger.

"If we don't do this just right, the spirits from beyond won't talk to us, or maybe they will come after us. So do everything I tell you just the way I tell you," she said. "Now, close your eyes and touch your knees together, and you can't peek or they won't come."

This was starting to get serious. Palms were becoming a little sweatier, and knees had the slightest tremble to them. Each kid's breathing became just a little more deliberate. They seemed to be making sure that each breath counted because they weren't sure when they would get to breathe again.

Then Granny started, "Spirits, are ya there?" Then very quietly to her friends, "Don't move or open your eyes, 'cause it may take several tries for us to contact them"

"Spirits, are ya there?" Just a little louder and with more authority.

A slight pause. The breathing of each child on that porch was now quite audible; you could practically hear their hearts pounding in the chests. Palms were practically dripping, and that slight tremble in the knees became much more noticeable.

"Spirits, are ya there?"

BANG! BANG! BANG!

Three loud bangs thundered from the porch. All eyes opened, all breathing stopped, replaced by screaming. Simultaneously, the porch was cleared while children ran screaming across the field in front of the house, feet barely touching the ground and nearing the point of loss of bladder control. All, that is, except for Granny.

Granny just sat on the porch, rolled her eyes in disgust, and said, "Daddy." Then, as if on cue from under the porch she began to hear the laughing of her father.

Paw Paw was a joker. He loved to play pranks and cut up. Everyone who knew Paw Paw knew this well. The legends of his practical jokes probably still live at Texas A&M, almost a hundred years after he went there. This summer night in Texas, however, he was in his prime and couldn't miss an opportunity like this.

Unknown to Granny, Paw Paw had been able to listen to everything she and her friends had been saying. There was no background highway noise or any city noise. It was simply a small wooden house on a prairie with all the windows open in order to keep as cool as possible. In this setting, sound carries very well. From his vantage point in his bed, Paw Paw could hear every word they said. When Granny started to tell them about the séance, his mental wheels began to turn, and his more devious side took over.

As Granny prepared her friends for the séance, Paw Paw, still in his nightclothes, climbed out of his bedroom window. He then quietly crawled under the house as Granny was beginning to tell them to close their eyes and touch their knees together. By the time she was starting to call out to the spirits, Paw Paw was directly under them with rock in hand ready to act. He patiently waited for just the right moment. Even from his vantage point, under the porch, he could hear their breathing reaching a fever pitch. Just after Granny called to the spirits the third time, Paw Paw knew the time was right and he took the rock in his hand and rapped it against the floor joist of the porch.

After Paw Paw climbed out from under the porch, he gave Granny a big hug. Granny, although a little bitter towards Paw Paw, was biting her tongue to prevent herself from laughing. Although she found it just as humorous as Paw Paw did, she didn't want to admit it. Eventually, she loosened up and was able to appreciate the moment with her father. However, I believe after the run her friends had it took them slightly longer to find the humor in the whole situation that Granny and Paw Paw did.

A Bucket of Oil

Samuel took a vial of oil and poured it on his head, and kissed him; he said, "The LORD has anointed you ruler over his people Israel. You shall reign over the people of the LORD and you will save them from the hand of their enemies all around. Now this shall be the sign to you that the LORD has anointed you ruler over his heritage.

1 Samuel 10:1

In ancient Israel when a king was selected, as part of his coronation, he was anointed by pouring oil over his head representing the fact that he was the Lord's anointed for a particular ministry, that of leading God's people. Samuel anointed Saul as the first king of Israel to be that leader of God's people as their king. The same occurred with David and all subsequent kings of Israel from that time on.

In Holy Baptism we too are anointed for a particular ministry, that of serving God and making disciples; we too are God's anointed. However, Messiah is the Hebrew word for "God's anointed;" the equivalent Greek word is Christ. Now we are not THE Messiah or THE Christ, but we are God's anointed for ministry in this world.

When I was very young I didn't really understand the concept of God's anointed, or even what it meant to be anointed with oil. There are many things you do in life that seem prophetic and point to things later in life. I suppose that being a pastor now I could make a reach that I was anointing myself for later ministry, but that reach is probably a bit too far. More often than not when a three-year-old is involved it is not very prophetic, but simply boiled down to, "he's three."

Life on a farm and the rest of the world seem to have nothing in common. Farm life is very simple, and simple methods are maintained. For much of my life, I remember that the road on which the family farm sits was a dusty, dry, dirt road. To this day, the water on that family farm comes from a private well. It is a relaxing life on that farm, with no pretension or desire for it, and certainly no equal. Until recently, most rooms were heated by fireplaces or wood burning stoves. It is not a large house, but it was able to house my grandparents and five children. It is not uncommon now that you will find the remaining members of that family still gathered around the kitchen table, with children, grandchildren, and a growing list of great-grandchildren testing the loving flexibility of those walls.

Just because it is a magical place does not imply that that no work occurred there; far from it. Life on that farm meant hard work and lots of it. Nothing was wasted. Very little was thrown away. What little trash that remained was burned in a barrel beside the garden then the ashes tilled into the garden. Kitchen waste was either given to the dogs and cats or used to compost the garden. Even the oil from the lawn mowers and tractors was reused.

Although the EPA would probably not approve, nothing associated with that household ever truly went to waste. In those days it was quite common to take the spent oil and sprinkle it on the driveway and roadway to keep dust down, since it was not yet paved. This was done in somewhat of a feeble effort to reduce the amount of dust permeating the house, requiring daily dusting of nearly every surface in the house. What exacerbated the situation in that house was the fact that a sawmill also was on that road and daily logging and lumber trucks made their way up and down the road, raising dust in biblical proportions.

Papaw never did get very far beyond keeping his life and needs very simple. He never even saw the need for fancy oil drain pans. Instead he used old paint cans, over and over again. Now to a three-year-old, this is simply another toy, as is everything encountered at that age.

After the oil was drained into the paint cans he would leave them sitting in the car shed (some people may refer to this as a garage, but to us it is the car shed) until he was ready to use it. The oil itself had the consistency of blackstrap molasses, and easily had as much as 10,000 miles or more on it by the time he would change it. Papaw was frugal even in his changing of the oil, and did not want to do it too often.

Since I was the first grandchild, nothing had been put up yet, and who would have ever thought that I would even be interested in a paint can of oil. Besides, a gallon can of spent oil weighs about 10 pounds, fully 1/3 of my weight at the time. Even if I was interested in it, I wasn't likely to be able to move it. Nevertheless, I was interested and I could move it. Not only could I move it, but I could also lift it.

It is odd what you remember through the passage of time, but I still remember, to this day, the pungent, acrid, sulfurous smell of that used oil, mixing with the unmistakable scent of dry, dusty earth. Despite the accuracy and detail of my memory, I am still not sure what possessed me to take the next action I did. I can't fathom the logic in it, or even how I could have been curious about it in this way. I certainly didn't know what oil was, nor did I have any concept of just how dirty it was. To me it was simply the black stuff in the cans. It felt kind of gooey and sticky. Maybe even the same consistency as the gooey and sticky stuff that Mommy would put on my head when I had a bath. Plus, once you have a little on your chubby little fingers after putting your hand down in it, what the heck it could easily do the same now as what Mommy would do, and not even need your bath later.

Yes that's right; I upended the entire can of oil on my head. I can still remember the slime of it running down over my head and body. This was absolutely hilarious, and I began to laugh hysterically. I giggled and laughed and went to find Mommy. I am sure at that point I could only be described as something that resembled Brer Rabbit's tar baby. However, Mommy did not see the humor in it that I did.

In the middle of running about and destroying some good clothes, my mother stripped me naked in the yard and took the garden hose to me; that just made it even better. I loved playing in the water, and I guess Mommy did too! I played and splashed, and danced around naked in the yard. Life should always be that good. Can't you just imagine all of us today, covered in motor oil and running through the sprinkler in the backyard naked; you really can't go back to being three again. Just as all this was going on, the new pastor pulled up in the driveway to make his first visit to our quaint family farm.

The tradition, at that time, was when a new pastor arrived he would drive around to each of the parishioners' homes to visit his new congregation. It would be impossible to know exactly what was going through the new pastor's mind as he watched a frantic mother, chasing a naked boy covered in oil with a garden hose, and a grandmother with a towel in her hands laughing hysterically. Of all the classes that I took in seminary myself I can honestly say that none of them addressed what to say or do on your first encounter with a family and find a mother chasing a naked boy covered in motor oil with a garden hose. What can you possibly say at a point like that other than, "Hi, I'm Pastor Homer Barker, your new pastor." However, this scene would certainly leave an indelible mark on a person; something that no seminary ever really prepares a pastor for.

Mamaw was a tall slender woman, and there was never any doubt in my mind that she thoroughly loved me. She laughed and laughed as I danced around while Mommy sprayed me with the garden hose. Then she met me on the steps to the back porch with a nice warm towel when Mommy was done. She beckoned to the pastor to join us inside for a cup of coffee and a good laugh, as she wrapped the towel around me with her loving arms. She laughed with me a bit, and then took me for a nice warm bath. Life should always be that good.

Milking Time

Rid yourselves, therefore, of all malice, and all guile, insincerity, envy, and all slander. Like newborn infants, long for the pure, spiritual milk, so that by it you may grow into salvation— if indeed you have tasted that the Lord is good.

1 Peter 2:1-3

For a number of years my grandparents raised dairy cattle. To be honest, they gave up dairy cattle when my uncle Joe graduated from high school and the labor for milking the cows went off to college. For a couple of years after that they maintained a herd of dairy cattle that required milking every day. But, the labor required for a couple in their fifties was more than my grandparents were prepared for. They were preparing for retirement, not adding more work.

Running a dairy farm is very rewarding, but it is also very labor intensive. Each cow requires milking twice a day. The milk has to be gathered and stored until either you take it to the dairy or they come and pick it up. Each of the milk cans holds about 5 gallons of milk, and therefore weighs about 60 pounds. More often than not, my grandmother was stuck with that task.

Many people may not realize it, but dairy cattle are creatures of habit. Once they establish which stall they will be milked in, that is the only stall they will go to. When it is milking time, they are more than anxious to get milked; as the milk builds up in them, so does the pressure. It is as if they have to go to the bathroom, very bad, and you are their only outlet. It is not difficult to get them to love you under these circumstances. They stand at the gate waiting on you to bring them in for milking. Usually, they almost charge the gate because they are so bloated and uncomfortable. Their schedule is inviolate, and they will be ready, on time, even if you are not.

I loved to participate in the daily events around the farm, and although I was not really old enough or large enough, I would often attempt to help. More often than not, this help turned out to be more of a chore for everyone else than assistance.

One day, my grandmother was milking the cows and I was observing; or at least I was supposed to be only observing. Somehow,

I got it in my head that she needed assistance. The best way I could think of to help was to bring her another cow. After all, the cows were there, I was there, and they needed milking. What could go wrong?

Despite my age and very small stature, somehow I found a way to release the gate latch and coax another cow out. This in and of itself was no small task. No gate on the farm was as straightforward at a normal gate with just a quick latch and some well-oiled hinges. Most of them were cedar posts with barbed wire running between them with no support between the cedar posts. To open the gate you had to release the catch then drag the first cedar post around with the barbed wire and other post in the center dragging along behind you. The closure point had a ring made of wire at the bottom that was semi-fixed and one at the top that was capable of slipping over the top of the moveable post. How I did this is still beyond me. As I mentioned, I was only three and maybe three feet tall if I put a little newspaper in my shoes. The loop at the top had to be moved up to open the gate and it rested at about four and a half feet off the ground. I had to move this loop up to about five feet to get the gate open. Nevertheless, I did it.

Once the task of opening the gate was behind me all I had to do now was to convince one of the cows to come with me to be milked next. What I did not count on was the fact that the one cow I invited had friends who also wanted to be milked; now. By the time my grandmother realized what was happening, I had cows all over the yard. It is hard to imagine why, but she really didn't find much humor in this situation.

My grandmother came out of the milk house shouting and running around chasing about five cows back into the fenced in area until she was ready for them. I probably was not supposed to be amused by this, but boy was I. Now I knew I had something that I could help her with. It is truly amazing how fast a cow can run. We chased them and chased them until we finally got them back in the pin. There is no doubt in my mind that as she would get one cornered, my attempts at assistance only freed that cow again. I have no idea how long this all took. After all, I was only three and the concept of time to a three-year-old doesn't hold a lot of water. Eventually, we did get the cows back to where they belonged.

Milking Time

After all of the excitement, I got a severe scolding from my grandmother. This kind of took me by surprise. This woman, who had only shown me love in large quantities was now scolding me over helping her. However, never was I scolded there without also being hugged and told how much I was loved. Looking back years later, I understood perfectly how dangerous what I had done was. But, we all know what the word danger means to a three-year-old. Nuclear physics means just about as much at that time. I do remember recognizing, even at that early age, what I had done was wrong then. Because of the love my grandmother had shown in the way she scolded me, I also understood that my grandmother was not asking me to not do something because she was being vindictive, but because she loved me and was concerned about my wellbeing; not to mention how hard recalcitrant cows are to round back up.

Grandparents are great for teaching right from wrong. They aren't concerned about anything but loving you and making sure that you are safe. There is never a doubt to a child that their grandparent loves them and is not doing this to them to be mean. The distance they have from you is sufficient that it is not the same that is felt when a parent tries to teach you the exact same lesson. The lessons that my grandmother taught me, are to this day indelible in my mind.

A Doorknob for a Toy

The Lord will guide you continually, and satisfy your needs in parched places, and
make your bones strong; and you shall be like a watered garden, like a spring of
water, whose waters never fail.

Isaiah 58:11

Most kids live for the most expensive toys advertised. They want
the Snoopy Sno Cone Machine, the Easy Bake Oven, the Deluxe Hot
Wheels set, the Arctic Adventure GI Joe Set. Yet most kids end up
playing with the box the toy came in as much as they do they toy.
You can play with as expensive of a toy as you want, but you always
come back to the simple pleasures in life. Even when you get older
that doesn't seem to go away.

When I was younger, I was no different. I wanted the expensive
bicycles, the GI Joe that talks – with the beard of course, and the
deluxe chemistry set. I played with all of it, but I also played with the
box. I remember very vividly when our parents got a new freezer my
sister and I played with the cardboard box that the freezer came in for
at least a week. We played with that box until it was almost
unrecognizable as a box.

Living with Granny and Granddaddy for about a year, they got to
know my sister and I very well. Granny knew just how to make the
smiley face pancakes and Granddaddy knew how everything worked.
They both began to pick up on mine and my sister's likes and dislikes.
They began to understand what truly appealed to us, and made sure
that we were able to enjoy some of these things. My sister loved her
dolls, and anything that would enhance her appearance. Granny
would take the time to brush her hair, and let her wear some costume
jewelry earrings. Granny really took the time to make sure that she
felt special.

I, on the other hand, had a tendency to take things apart. I had a
tremendous fascination with what makes things tick. Of course, if
you ask my wife today, that fascination has not diminished in the
least. Today I am usually able to put something back together again,
and it actually works. However, at the age of 6 all of the screws

seemed like a bit of an overkill; I was quite sure that all of the parts were not entirely necessary.

At one point I had a small robot that I really enjoyed playing with until the batteries died. I wasn't convinced that the reason for its demise was the fact that the batteries died, so I proceeded to dissect my robot to find out what was "wrong" with him. Unfortunately, he did not survive the surgery any better than the previous ten items that I had dismantled to find out what was "wrong" with them. I imagine that this trend was beginning to concern my grandparents, and out of a sense of self-defense they needed to give me items that didn't really matter if I was able to reassemble them or not.

Granddaddy had recently replaced some of the doorknobs around the house, and really had no use for the discarded ones, but I did. He gave me one of the dull brass door knobs to play with. Within minutes I had begun to disassemble it. I really dove into it taking out all of the intricate pieces and asking Granddaddy what each of them were; I am still amazed at his patience. With each screw, nut, bolt, and locking mechanism I began to uncover the mysteries of how door knobs and locking mechanisms work.

Hours and hours I sat quietly with my doorknob assembling and disassembling to find out how the pieces worked together. I removed all of the pieces I could and put them back together to see how they interacted with each other. I was completely and totally enthralled with this simple machine. My grandparents were completely at ease with the fact that I was not trying to disassemble the refrigerator to find out how it worked. As a result, the secret was out of the bag now.

For years after this, my parents, grandparents, aunts, uncles, and anyone else who valued their functioning equipment would give me things that were broken to fix; especially if they did not really care if it got repaired or not. Sometimes the patient would survive and sometimes it wouldn't. As I got older, oddly enough, more of them survived than didn't. Just to think, it all started with my grandparents paying attention to what appealed to me and building on it.

Eventually, this interest turned into a college degree and a job as an engineer for a number of years. I tinkered, disassembled, and reassembled a multitude of things during the years that I worked as an engineer. Although I no longer work as an engineer the drive to see what makes things tick is still very much alive and well within me. I doubt seriously if I have taken a doorknob apart in decades, but should the need arise I feel ready.

Chute-a-par

Thus says the Lord of hosts: Old men and old women shall again sit in the streets of Jerusalem, each with staff in hand because of their great age. And the streets of the city shall be full of boys and girls playing in its streets.

Zechariah 8:4-5

Granny was one of the craftiest people I ever met. Never did we visit her without some craft-type project being presented to us. Usually, they were quite fun, and often they would be based around our faith and the church. I have no doubt that many of her projects, out of a sense of self-preservation, were to keep us out of trouble, but with her it was mostly just for fun. There was even an occasion where she took me along in my teens to visit a nursing home where she volunteered with the residents there to do crafts; everyone did crafts with Granny no matter how old or young they were.

One of the homes that she and my grandfather lived in was a split-level with a large wooden porch on the back. Descending down from the porch via the stairs would put you in the midst of a large, grassy back yard bordered on the back side by a small stream. One of the little "projects" that Granny dreamed up for me was fishing in that stream. Never mind the fact that the stream wasn't large enough for most minnows, much less a fish, but when you have imagination who needs reality?

From among the various limbs that I found in the back yard, Granny helped me to select an appropriate "fishing pole". We took it back to the house and tied a piece of fishing line to it. Now, being four years old I really didn't understand the difference between fishing line and binders' twine, and I definitely did not understand what difference it made to the fish, so I went with it. Granny cut off about a 5 foot length of binders twine and affixed it to the end of my "fishing pole." Granny, in her infinite wisdom, convinced me that a hook probably wasn't necessary for fishing from her creek, so we didn't even look for something that would pass for a hook. As for bait, this was the most amusing part. Even at that point in the 1960's, many companies had adopted the practice of using foam peanuts for packaging material. To Granny, and to me, these had the oddly similar appearance to worms. Granny took one of my "worms" and tied it to the line, and now I was ready to fish.

I headed off across the back yard, and made my way to the small stream. To Granny's relief, I was quite content to sit and drown my "worm" in that small stream and while away the hours. I was able to just sit on the bank and enjoy life, at least until my attention span dissipated. Once that happened, which had to have been at least 10 minutes later, it was on again.

Funny thing about shallow streams; they are fun. I was able to climb around in the stream and turn over rocks looking for crawdads. I was able to see if I could find any other bait that may wriggle like what most people would call black snakes. I was able to test my immunity to poison ivy. At the end of it all, I was able to test the cleaning power of Granny's washing machine. I am glad to say that it had enough power for even my messes.

Visiting Granny and Granddaddy in that home I was introduced to one of my favorite people in the entire world, EVER, the ice cream man. For those who are unindoctrinated in the ways of the world, the ice cream man so totally rocks. I had never experienced such a phenomenon, a man who brings ice cream to you in a great big truck and a gazillion different flavors. My concept of what heaven must be like suddenly and unexpectedly exploded into reality.

We heard him coming from quite some distance long before we saw him. I had never heard that kind of music simply wafting through the neighborhood before. It was a tinkling and repetitive droning of "All Around the Mulberry Bush", and crazy loud.

Granny had pressed fifty cents into my grubby palm and had instructed me to go stand beside the road in front of her house. The sound of the music gradually increased in volume as the anticipated arrival of the ice cream man approached; it was torture, but I waited. Finally, there he came in a large white truck. Now, this was not the stereotypical ice cream truck of today that is a panel van with a large window in the back that the operator sticks his head through to ask what you want. Nope, this was a truck; a pickup truck with a big chest freezer in the back of it like you would have in a home.

The driver of the truck came to a halt directly in front of me and got out of his truck. He came around behind the truck and climbed up into it, but he did not turn off the truck or the music. Although I had no clue about why he left it all running at the time I do understand now; it was all to keep that massive freezer running. The engine roared and the music bellowed such that people in the neighboring county had no doubt the ice cream man was here.

My comprehension of the varieties of ice cream was limited, at best. My understanding of varieties was pretty much exhausted at vanilla, chocolate, and strawberry. Plastered on the side of his truck were pictures of such varieties and styles that my mind was well and truly blown. I was prepared to simply stand there and stare for hours until I finally made my choice; the ice cream man, however, was not.

He was gruff and just a bit impatient, and bellowed down to me to tell him what ice cream I wanted. With the sounds of the truck and the music I had no clue what he was yelling at me about so I replied with the typical reply of a four-year-old, "What?" My voice, however, was not the operatic voice of Pavarotti and did not carry far at all so a comedy of errors ensued where both of us are shouting back and forth to each other, "What!?!"

In frustration, my friend, the ice cream man, eventually shoved a cup of vanilla ice cream and a flat wooden spoon in my hand and took my fifty cents. Of course, that was an event in and of itself since I barely came to the top of the wheels in height and he could not lean over far enough to reach me. It required him to come down out of the back of the truck so that he and I were able to come in contact with each other. With ice cream in hand I left satisfied to return to Granny's house where she had been watching the entire event unfold with glee and not very well controlled laughter.

As I enjoyed my ice cream Granny prepared for the next craft that would hopefully keep me occupied for more than about ten minutes. Of course, I was completely oblivious to that fact because ice cream is just awesome. Once I did finish my ice cream, both the part that made it in me and the part that made it on me, I did require significant cleaning before Granny would be comfortable for me to participate in any activity, or touch anything in her house.

Once the prerequisites of cleaning were accomplished Granny gathered me up again, and sitting before here were the components necessary for our next activity. She had two handkerchiefs (well-used but clean), binder's twine, and a rock. Although it may sound like the beginning of a great joke or an episode of MacGyver it really did produce and awesome craft.

Granny had me place the rock in the center of one of the handkerchiefs and pull the sides up around it. Then, with significant help from Granny, we tied 4 pieces of the binder's twine to the now weighted handkerchief. Then each of those pieces of twine were connected to each of the four corners of the second handkerchief. It was probably the simplest and quickest craft I had ever done with her; I had fully expected to be at it for hours (not that I really understood what an hour was). But, we actually were done in all of about 10 minutes.

With the completed craft in hand she escorted me to the back yard and had me throw my new project into the air. That should have been the easy part, but it still took me several tries to get it off the ground. Once successfully launched the craft sailed into the air then the assembled projected lightly floated back to the ground since my parachute had opened. This was AWESOME!!

For the next hour plus, I launched and relaunched my parachute repeatedly with an extreme amount of glee. With an uncle in the Army, I had romanticized what it means to be in the military, and envisioned him parachuting into his objective over and over again with soldierly precision and expertise. Granny had no idea that this would be such an incredible toy for me, but she struck pay dirt with this one; I was occupied for a significant amount of time.

Later on that afternoon my parents came to retrieve my sister and me from our grandparents and I was still enthralled with my new toy, and especially the fact that I had made it (truth be told I think I actually watched it being made but in my mind I made it).

As my mother came through the door to greet my sister and me, I came rushing at her with my new toy in hand, "Mommy, Mommy, Mommy look!! I made a chute-a-par!!" This was exclaimed as I ran through the house hoisting my new toy in my hand, grubby with the dirt from the back yard, and with barely enough time for my mother to stop me from wrapping the same grubby hands around her.

My mother looked to her mother, my Granny, to figure out what on earth I was talking about. Granny was barely able to contain her laughter and she explained over me that it was actually a parachute, not a chute-a-par. My mother never missed a beat and quickly applauded me for the great job that I had done.

Of the experiences during that particular stay with my grandmother the thing that still sticks out to me the most is not the gift in the form of crafts, nor the great food, nor even the ability to get away with a little more than I normally would have at home. No, the greatest gift was her time. She spent time with me, one on one and gave me herself and her love. I walked away that day with memories that lasted many times longer than my chute-a-par ever would.

Corn on the Cob

When I was a child, I spoke like a child, I thought like a child, I reasoned like a child; when I became an adult, I put an end to childish ways.

1 Corinthians 13.11

I have often tried to convince myself that I have indeed put an end to childish ways, and become an adult. Maybe when I retire I will actually convince myself of that. I thought when I was younger that I would begin to feel like an adult when I turned 18 – that came and went with no success. Perhaps then when I got married – we still enjoy just playing together. Maybe I needed to be a father first – it is truly hard to resist a three-year-old when she wants you to play dress up with her. I guess I may never grow up, and that is OK for me. When I was 51, I would often hear my daughter say, "Mom, Dad lost his one." What she was implying is that I was no longer acting 51, but 5.

There is a lot about being a child, especially a child of God, which makes the world around you just fine. The only problem is, I don't always comprehend things as an adult when I live like a child, but I am getting there.

Sometimes the simplest of events can be traumatic for a three-year-old; take, for instance, your average ear of corn. Do you remember the first time you discovered that corn may or may not be on the cob when it is time to eat it? I had been spoiled and sheltered for many years. I took for granted that corn came on cobs and that was the only way that you would find it. You can imagine my horror when I discovered that some people may choose to cut the corn off the cob and do it intentionally. It scarred me for life.

My grandparents were denture wearers, and as a result they really could not eat corn on the cob. Now to comprehend this delicate subject at the age of three is no simple task. In my world there were certain unalterable facts, and chief among those was the fact that corn was meant to be on the cob.

Mamaw and Papaw always had their own garden and plenty of fresh vegetables; even our large family could never possibly eat as much as that garden produced on our own. The beefsteak tomatoes were always plump and ripe. The blue lake green beans were crisp and juicy. The luscious turnips with their purple cap had just enough bite to be just right, and were fragrant as you sliced them open to enjoy one fresh from the ground. However, my favorite was always the corn on the cob. It could be yellow or white; I didn't care what the variety was or how large of an ear it was. I simply loved the precious sweetness that can only seem to be found in fresh homegrown corn.

Mamaw's kitchen was relatively small, but somehow seemed to hold as many people as necessary, no matter what the occasion. There was just enough room in the middle of the floor for a rather plain, rectangular, Formica top table with six chairs. Around the perimeter were a series of wooden cabinets, which to me each contained their own separate treasures. In the small drawer beside the sink was an abundance of treasures just waiting for me to discover them. It didn't seem to matter that I had explored that exact same drawer only last week; I simply must see if there were any new treasures. In these treasure chests of mine I found pocket knives from many different decades, pennies and other odd change, wing nuts to equipment that had been thrown away ten years before, and many other items that caught my curiosity. I just knew that this drawer was the key to solving the secrets of the universe; once I figured out what a universe was I would have the problem solved.

On one countertop was a pull out ceramic enamel metal work surface; I've never seen another one quite like it. The primary purpose for this work surface that I ever witnessed was making biscuits and boy could Mamaw make biscuits. Mamaw always made her biscuits from scratch, and there was no need in even discussing the Pillsbury Doughboy with her. She carefully assembled her ingredients with no recipe, no measuring cup, and no real careful thought. Well, I do have to make one correction to that statement. In the large metal tin that housed the flour for making the biscuits was an old aluminum single cup measuring cup. She used this cup for scooping out the flour, but I am confident that no actual measuring took place in the scooping of the flour. It was simply a matter of using the amount that felt right.

The recipe had really become second nature to her. She kneaded the dough with her hands and plopped it out onto that work surface to cut the biscuits. Mamaw never used one of those fancy store bought biscuit cutters; she just used a standard drinking tumbler upside down. During the process, Mamaw would recombine the dough about three times until she only had a small misshapen piece that she explained to me would go to the cat.

During the summer, the green beans were always fresh. They would come fresh from the garden; get a quick rinse then snapped straight into the pot. Not that it was very healthy for you, but the green beans always included a healthy chunk of fat back for seasoning. Healthy or not they were delicious, and we loved them.

My seat was always to Papaw's right. He always sat at the head of the table next to the sink. Since I was only three, my feet did not touch the floor yet and I had a tendency to swing my feet unconsciously. Inevitably I would end up kicking Papaw repeatedly. He would tell me to stop swinging my feet, and for at least a minute I would oblige until I absentmindedly began to swing them again. To me, sitting next to Papaw was a place of high honor. I was able to have more of his attention than just about anyone else. No other seat in that room was as important as the one to Papaw's right. I just loved talking with him and the way that he lovingly reminded me (over and over again) to stop swinging my feet. Periodically he would reach over with his rough leathery hands and ruffle my hair. At breakfast I was always fascinated, sitting next to him, why he drank his coffee from a small bowl instead of from a cup. He would get his coffee in a cup with a small bowl under it instead of a saucer. Then he would pour some of his coffee into the bowl and drink it. Of course, he was Papaw and if he did it then it must be cool.

Normally, I would hang around under foot as each meal was prepared, and I was stepped on more than once. It all seemed so simple to me. You cut it in pieces, you beat on it, you put a little flour on it, and then you fry it. It didn't really seem to matter what we were eating, it somehow followed that pattern. Sometimes one or more steps were skipped, but rarely was the frying step skipped. If that is all there is to it then I knew that I could do it.

Certain dishes were sacrosanct, and were not to be disturbed. This included biscuits – although you did have the option of honey or molasses, country ham, grits, and corn on the cob. The biscuits were light and fluffy, even though they did not come from a can.

From my uncles I learned the technique of eating copious quantities of biscuits with either honey or molasses. As I think back about that now I cannot begin to fully appreciate the number of biscuits that I would consume at one sitting; it was simply biblical in proportion. I would put a pat of butter onto my plate followed by pouring out over the butter either honey or molasses. The technique of pouring out the honey and molasses was a time-proven method that had been passed down from generation to generation and perfected as it went. First you tilt the jar until you get a nice even ribbon flowing of the sweet viscous nectar of the gods. Then, at just the right moment, you quickly right the jar and slide a case knife across the mouth of the jar, severing the ribbon of goodness and cutting off the flow. This acts to stop the flow and keep the jar clean so that you can actually open it the next time you want some. With that technique perfected it always amazed me how little honey or molasses dribbled down the side of the jar.

In my world, corn on the cob was as much of a ritualistic part of a meal as the biscuits and honey. You would take your cob of corn and slather enough butter on it to clog even the purest of arteries. Then you would lightly salt the cob as you turned it in your hand. The part about lightly salting took me years to get right; inevitably I would end up with one part that was as salty as a cow's salt lick. Eating the corn became its own art form to me. Sometimes I would eat as if I were running a typewriter; I would eat completely across one row at a time before starting another row. Other times I would eat in circles around the cob before working my way down. Still others I would pick out a zigzag pattern or draw pictures in the ear with my teeth. I found that there was no wrong way to eat an ear of corn.

However sacred the ear of corn was, Mamaw violated it. I will never forget the horror of finding a pile of little yellow buds on my plate. I had no idea of what it was, but I knew that it didn't look very appealing. I asked what it was and was told that it was corn. I just knew that they had lost their mind because there was no way that this pile of yellow stuff was corn. I asked why it was off the cob because corn was always on the cob. Now my family had the unique task of explaining to me what dentures were and how they reacted with corn on the cob – another foreign concept. Of course, Papaw pulled his teeth out of his pocket to show me since he never actually wore them; that blew my mind.

Mamaw tried, man did she ever try. I fought her tooth and nail. There was no way that she was going to convince me that this pile of yellow stuff was corn. I just simply wasn't buying it. However, out of a spirit to humor them, I tried it. It certainly tasted like corn, but I couldn't draw pictures in it. I was crushed. How could they take my corn off the cob? I demanded that they put my corn back on the cob. Now it was getting ugly. This one sent me into a fury. I couldn't believe that they had cut the corn off my cob – that's just wrong.

Years later, in my teens after the trauma I had experienced of having my corn removed from the cob, Papaw took me over to one of his neighbor's homes, Fred. Our job for the day was to help out Fred some on his farm and in return we would go back with a pickup truck load of old corn stalks to feed to the cows. As we headed out into Fred's garden area we hacked, and we cut, and we pulled for hours. Actually, as I now recall it, I believe I hacked, and cut, and pulled and Fred and Papaw supervised. Papaw was a master at the Tom Sawyer gifts of leadership to convince other people to do things they wouldn't normally do.

After we had been at it for a while Fred called me over to him, and beside him was a stalk still producing corn. He reached over and selected one of the ears of corn on that old stalk and pulled it right off. He inspected it – more or less – and pulled back the shucks, dusted off some of the silks and handed it to me, "Here, eat that boy."

I wasn't sure that he realized a simple fact, so I thought that I would remind him, "But it ain't cooked yet."

"Son, the good Lord is done with it, so you take a big ol' bite and enjoy," Fred retorted.

So I did, and he was so right. It was sweet and juicy. The white pearls of corn glistened in the sunlight as I bit into it over and over again. The juices ran down my chin, and I glimpsed a part of heaven that few ever experience but everyone should. Sitting in an open field with a summer breeze and eating corn on the cob that was still growing less than a minute before; that is a new level of ecstasy. This experience deepened my resolve about corn belonging on the cob, and it took some time, but I finally relented; I think that I was about thirty or so then. I have finally come to grips with the fact that it is ok to eat your corn not on the cob, but I still don't like it. I have thought of leading a national revolt to get laws passed about cutting the corn off of cobs, but I don't think that I will get much of a following. I suppose for now, I will just have to live with the excuse of dentures and only draw my pictures when my corn comes on the cob. But as for me and my house, we will eat our corn on the cob.

Doughboy

Who could ever forget the Pillsbury Doughboy - the cute, chubby, pasty white mascot for Pillsbury? I loved that little guy. I couldn't wait to see commercials come on where he popped from the can of biscuit dough. His adorable laugh made me laugh and giggle with delight every time I saw him. And, Granny killed him!!!

When I was only 3 or 4 the division between the real world and the imagined world was not very clearly defined. I lived in a world that if it was on TV then it must be real, and alive. In my world at that time were my friends Mr. Rogers, Captain Kangaroo, Ronald McDonald, and Bozo the Clown. I was convinced that somewhere in the phonebook (if I could read) that Bozo the Clown would be listed. One of my absolute favorites though was the Pillsbury Doughboy. I longed to be able to meet him someday and poke his little tummy.

As the commercial went, a lady on TV would be preparing a meal for her family; this was, of course, because men were incapable of performing such a task. During the course of the preparation, she would take out a can of Pillsbury biscuits, proudly display them so the entire world could see, and pop them on the countertop to open them. Then a little magic would occur with the satisfying pop of the can; the Pillsbury Doughboy would miraculously appear from the opening in the can. This I knew to be fact, since it was on TV.

I tried and I tried to get my mom to get some Pillsbury biscuits. I really wanted to see that little guy pop out. However, Mom, for some reason, always made her own biscuits. To me this was completely illogical. How on earth were you supposed to see the little white pasty guy if you didn't buy the biscuits? Besides, they were supposed to be just about the best biscuits in the world. However, Mom persisted in making her own. It is almost as if my rationale did not carry any weight with her, but that certainly could not have been the case.

Visiting Granny was a special treat for my sister and me. Granny always had special games and treats for us. We would always make or do something fun, and we were treated like we were the only kids in the world. We lived quite some distance from Granny, at that time, so we didn't get to see her very often, but it was so nice when we did.

On one trip to Granny's she was making us dinner when we arrived. Granny had a special table for my sister and I that was just the right height. It was a small, red, folding card table that could not have been more than two feet high, complete with matching folding metal chairs. My sister, Karen, and I would enjoy sitting at that table since we did not have to sit on the Sears & Roebuck catalog when we sat there in order to reach our food. Part of the preparation for dinner was biscuits, and Granny had the Pillsbury can of biscuits. I could hardly wait. I darted around the kitchen with baited anticipation. I just knew that finally I was going to get to see the Pillsbury Doughboy, and poke his chubby little tummy. I could already hear his infectious laugh.

Finally, Granny raised the tube of biscuits to strike it on the counter. I watched with eyes as large as silver dollars as the can struck the edge of the counter. I heard a satisfying pop, and saw the can part to reveal the already prepared biscuits inside the can. Then, to my amazement, Granny simply twisted the can further open and began to peel the raw biscuit dough from the can and put it on a cooking sheet. Nothing! Absolutely nothing else happened! There was No doughboy, No laughter, No giggling; Nothing!

Could I have missed him when he jumped out? After all, he did seem to be pretty quick. I didn't even hear him giggle. Granny did strike the counter pretty hard. She must have struck the counter harder than she should have and … and … she killed him! I was devastated. Granny killed the Pillsbury Doughboy!!

I was visibly shaken. I sobbed openly, and quite audibly. My Granny had just killed the little guy. I wasn't able to poke his little belly. I couldn't play with him. This was a tragedy of epic proportion.

Granny and my mom both recognized that I did not take this very well. Granny bent down and took me in her arms. She held me close and told me that it would all be ok, and tried as best she could to explain that the Pillsbury Doughboy was only on TV. That part she wasn't going to convince me of, because I knew the TV was real. They both assured me that Granny had not killed the Pillsbury Doughboy, and that everything was going to be ok; I just wasn't buying it.

For years, this event became a defining point in my life. I was forever and always connected now with the Pillsbury Doughboy. Even my giggle somehow seems to mimic his. My wife now believes that I am the doughboy incarnate. It is difficult now for a birthday, Christmas, or even anniversary to go by without someone giving me a Pillsbury Doughboy shirt, tie, doll, or other trademark item. And, I love it. He still makes me laugh, and he still makes me cry. His chubby little face will always be identified for me with my Granny, her love for me, and the day she killed him.

Freshly Ironed Clothes

O God, from my youth you have taught me, and I still proclaim your wondrous deeds.

Psalm 71:17

Much of what we experience as children is in preparation for adulthood. We learn to eat on our own, we learn to bathe on our own, we learn to dress on our own, etc. Sometimes we learn these skills from our parents, or from our friends, or from other relatives, or a combination. Sometimes, we even learn by trial and error.

As a child, I was always quite curious about various activities, and how they were done. I guess I looked at things much the same way that the boys passing by Tom Sawyer thought that the fence he was painting was a fun job. Honestly, I never knew if it was fun or not, but I was ready to experience it.

One day, while watching Granny iron, I experienced that sense of wonder, and I asked her, "Granny, what' cha doin'?"

"Well, John David, I am ironing clothes."

"Why ya' doin' that?"

"So your Granddaddy will have pressed clothes to go to work in."

"Right, what's pressed clothes?"

It is easy for any layman to see that this could be a never-ending saga for my grandmother. Only the wisest of grandparents are able to maneuver from this tricky hold by a five-year-old without bloodshed. Luckily, Granny was a shaman grand master at this art. In another setting, some would have referred to her as Master Yoda.

"John David, would you like for me to show you how to iron your clothes?" Granny asked this knowing that I was bound to take the bait; Granny was skilled well beyond her years.

"Sure Granny, that sounds like fun." I was hooked like a fine rainbow trout, with no chance of escape.

Granny took the time to get my sister's play iron and ironing board out. She carefully showed me how to iron then fold my clothes. She painstakingly pointed out that I should not leave the iron in one place for too long, and that I needed to iron both the front and the back of each of my tee shirts. Never mind that the iron I was using was as cold as a cucumber since it was not capable of producing any dangerous heat. What was especially wise on the part of the manufacturer of the toy iron is the fact that they did not even have a cord on the iron that I certainly would have tried to plug in.

Each item, I carefully ironed, then folded, and placed into my drawer. I worked beside Granny as she ironed my grandfather's shirts and pants, ironing my tee shirts. We both worked for some time, and eventually our work was done. It was a very satisfying feeling, and I was proud of the work I had done.

I could not wait for my mother to get home from work so that I could show her all that I had accomplished. When she came through the door later that day, I accosted her and drug her off to see my handiwork. "Mommy, look at what Granny and me did today!"

While my mother tried to ascertain exactly what I was indicating that I had done, she was telling me how proud she was of me, all the while not really having a clue at what I had done. After all, it is not that common that a five-year-old little boy would be pointing to an open drawer full of clothes. With some additional guidance from my grandmother, it became a little clearer to my mom. "He worked all afternoon to iron his own clothes," my grandmother told her.

"Wow, you ironed these clothes all by yourself?!?" Obviously encouraging the tiny effort that I made, my mother wanted to keep this trend going for when heat was actually included in the ironing process.

As the rest of the evening progressed, my prowess with the iron became the continued topic for conversation. My pride in the job that I had done was bolstered throughout the evening, and I went to bed that night with my head in the clouds. Unfortunately, the rest of my body was not in the clouds with my head.

As a five-year-old little boy, I still had difficulty making it through the night without going to the bathroom; much like being in my fifties now. It was quite common for me to get up, find my way to the bathroom, do my business, return to my bed, and never really wake up. To help me make this journey without incident, my grandmother had placed a nightlight in the bathroom to guide my cobweb-filled head like a ship to a lighthouse. This was a tradition that I had become used to, and comfortable with. Unfortunately, as of this night it was no longer the only nightlight in the house.

As an added effort to help me find my way around in the dark, Granny placed an additional nightlight in my bedroom. It was a considerate and loving move on the part of my grandmother, but unfortunately an additional lighthouse that guided me onto the rocks of destruction, which is actually what happens when a ship follows the light of a lighthouse.

When I got up that evening, it went according to my normal routine. My eyes were barely open. I followed my instincts and made my way to the bathroom. I lifted the seat, as I had been taught to do, and did my business. I then staggeringly made my way back to bed and continued sleeping for the rest of the night quite soundly.

I awoke in the morning and made my way to the breakfast table, where my Granny sat waiting on me. "Good morning sunshine, did you sleep well?"

"Yes, Granny," I answered, still rubbing the sleep from my eyes.

"Did you have to use the bathroom during the night?"

"I don't remember Granny, I may have." At five, my ability to remember and put together any significant events was not the most reliable in the world. As far as I knew, the world could have ended and begun again while I was sleeping.

"Well, John David, you did go to the bathroom last night, but not the normal way." Granny had gotten to the point that she could barely contain her laughter. She tried to be loving and compassionate, but her laughter was about to give her away. She related to me the story of what had actually happened the previous night.

With the new nightlight, my guidance system was not accurate enough to distinguish between one nightlight and another. My cobweb-filled head guided me instead of to the bathroom to the dresser in my bedroom. When I thought that I was lifting the toilette seat, I was opening the drawer. When I thought that I was filling the toilette, I was instead anointing my own clothing. I was too out of it to even realize that the clothes that I had just anointed were the ones that I had spent the time ironing earlier.

Granny related my faux pas to me, but never made me feel stupid. Instead, I felt nothing but the love of my grandmother. I knew that I had made a mistake, and Granny helped me to find a way to keep it from happening again. Never did I feel like she was making fun of me, even when she was laughing.

Picking a good climbing tree

He entered Jericho and was passing through it. A man was there named Zacchaeus; he was a chief tax-collector and was rich. He was trying to see who Jesus was, but on account of the crowd he could not, because he was short in stature. So he ran ahead and climbed a sycamore tree to see him, because he was going to pass that way. When Jesus came to the place, he looked up and said to him, 'Zacchaeus, hurry and come down; for I must stay at your house today.'

Luke 19:1-5

Many grandmothers are crafty, but Granny seemed to take it to a whole new level; she could make anything out of nothing at all, and make it look good. If anything was in any way crafty, she would give it a try. She tried her hand at papier mache, oil painting, pen and ink, charcoal, ceramic, decoupage, etc. She was an "equal opportunity" artist. Everything we experienced with her was an opportunity to explore, be creative, and especially learn more about various forms of art. If there was a 12-Step program for arts and crafts addicts, Granny should have been a charter member.

To Granny imagination was very important, and she did a lot to foster imagination in her grandchildren. She would help us make forts out of cardboard, fly our rocket ship to the moon in our little red wagon, and imagine what our lives would be like many years down the road. Our wildest dreams combined with hers were our only limitations, and there we inhabited a world without borders or limits. We could be anything and go anywhere. And that cardboard box would be transformed in our world to vast exploration of space and time; especially important in the 60's.

Moving into a new house as a child was traumatic, and Granny recognized this better than most people. While everyone around you is concerned about getting the power turned on or the phone connected, Granny was helping to pick out a good climbing tree. Not just any tree would do either.

Granny would sit with us as the entire world was changing around us. Yet, with Granny there we never even noticed. She would discuss each tree in our new yard with us. We would discuss what kind of tree it was, and weigh its many benefits for climbing. Limbs that were sturdy and reachable were important, but also sufficient height to see beyond our limited confines.

In the spring of 1969 my mother, sister, and I moved in with my grandparents where we took up residence for about the next year. This was not an easy move on anyone involved. This is where Granny's artistic side really helped to soften the blow and make the transition more palatable. For that year my sister and I made more crafts, did more drawings, and more paintings than we ever knew existed. It was amazing many years later when each of us discovered that Granny had kept most of that artwork for posterity and very sentimental reasons. We stayed continuously busy. However, one of the things that she introduced to me was a great climbing tree.

In our home we had previously lived in there was a tree bordering our house and our neighbor's; it was a large apple tree. It was filled with limbs that went in a myriad of different directions, each offering the opportunity to climb to different heights and gain different perspectives. From those limbs I could go anywhere and be anything, and I would spend hours in that tree. However, being an apple tree I was also able to enjoy one of my favorite fruits and never have to leave my "wooden fortress". In that incredible apple tree though I learned where my fantastic world of make-believe and the real world collided.

As a child, if one piece of chocolate is good then certainly ten pieces would be great; if one donut takes the edge off your hunger then after about twelve donuts you are satisfied completely. I applied the same logic to the apples in my apple tree; if one would be scrumptious then five would be over the moon. And, I was way over the moon stopping only when I reached about ten of those slightly tart and wonderful green apples. Oh yes, did I mention they were green? Well, they were, and I revisited those apples for many hours throughout that night because not only had I eaten way too many but they were green; not a lesson I plan on repeating – once was perfectly sufficient for a lifetime.

In the back of Granny's yard stood a line of a variety of different trees that bordered her property and the neighbor behind her. There, unfortunately, was no apple tree, but only a crab apple tree. Not only were its limbs pitifully small but so was its fruit with a flavor that would turn your mouth inside out with its tartness; I know this because I tried them. There was a pine tree, with great and mighty limbs, and enough pine sap to thoroughly destroy all my clothing. There were a couple of scrubby little trees that honestly looked more like bushes. In the midst of them all, though, there was one oak that was perfect.

It was sturdy with a glimmering gray bark. It had large limbs jutting out at just the right angles to gain a strong purchase and make my way up into its confines. I could climb up a few levels and gain a different perspective on the world or I could stay low on a limb that would hold me like I was in bed.

Granny explored that tree with me and helped me to ensure that it was the right tree for me and assess it for my purposes. It was perfect, and it offered me a refuge from which I was able to discern a world that had gone crazy. It was a place that I could climb to the stars and join the astronauts that had so frequently escaped the bonds of earth in the previous few years. It was just what I needed, and Granny helped me to find it.

About a year later, when my mother remarried, we moved into our new home about 30 minutes away. With Granny's encouragement, one of my first goals at our new home was to find my new tree. I eventually found several in the expanse of woods behind our house and across the street from it as well. However, my first foray into the selection of "my tree" was to a sad looking pine tree in our front yard.

This tree went up only about 8 or 10 feet before it started making a marked sweep out so that by the time you were only about 12 feet up the tree it was nearly parallel with the ground and just a few feet further it actually started pointing back to the ground. This, in no way, discouraged me from giving this tree a try.

I began to shimmy up the tree, and within just a few seconds had already reached the part where I was parallel with the ground. There were no limbs or anything to grab onto, but on I climbed. By the time I was up what should have been about 20 feet on the tree I was probably only 7 or 8 feet off the ground. That was actually quite fortunate because my grip slipped and I came crashing back to the ground flat on my back. Any air that may have been in my body was immediately expelled, and I quickly determined that just about any other tree would be a better choice. For the balance of the time we called that location our home I had a plethora of trees to choose from that worked well for my purposes; just not that one.

A Hammer and a Four-Year-Old

They surrounded me like bees; they blazed like a fire of thorns; in the name of the
Lord I cut them off!

Psalm 118:12

Grandparents are often overwhelmed by the boundless energy of their grandchildren. The result of this is that grandparents will not always make the soundest of decisions in their efforts to redirect some of that energy. Often they will agree to the most foolish things just to get them to quiet down. Other times they will try to find something to occupy the little nymph, even for just a moment while they get a few minutes off their feet. Sometimes this can be a rousing success. Sometimes, the grandparent will regret for years that foolish decision.

Cardboard boxes are on the list of huge success stories. I have often wondered who the first grandparent was that came up with the simple cardboard box as a toy. Perhaps it was Methuselah giving that first cardboard box to Noah; we all know how inspiring that was years later.

Granny was my inventive grandmother. She was absolutely fantastic at finding little games for us to play, and ways to make anything out of nothing. For inspiring imagination, she was tops. With Granny, no dream was too large and none was too small. She knew each of her grandchildren so well, and knew the best way to find appropriate entertainment for each of us, usually. I am confident that some of us provided a greater challenge for her than she was aiming for that day, but she still gave it a pretty good effort.

On one particular occasion, Granny gave me a small hammer to play with, and no real guidelines of what to and not to do; probably not one of her soundest moments. Granny, being an artist, often did her own framing. She had the miter boxes, and wire, and nails, and naturally the small hammers just right for assembling frames. Now Granny naturally thought that I could hardly get into any trouble with such a small hammer. So she handed it to me and sent me out onto the porch to hammer in any nails that may be sticking up a little on her porch. This was, of course, a job that needed to be done and with such a small hammer I could probably work all day on one nail and not get it done. What Granny didn't count on, however, was my short attention span.

I set out with my trusty hammer, and for a while I was "Little Joe" on the Ponderosa. It fit into my belt just perfectly to be my six-shooter. In my mind I had Joe's characteristic black hat on and rode that beautiful painted horse of his, which of course was a yardstick that Granny had turned into a pony with a newspaper head. I rode around for a while, chasing my sister, and practicing my draw; it was amazing at how often I was the quickest draw.

After a busy, at least ten minutes riding I was off to new adventures. The next adventure that I embarked on was discovering all of the really neat sounds that things would make when I struck them with the hammer. Most things on the back porch were wooden, but even they made some really neat sounds. I made my way around the porch to each new item, rapping on it several times, thoroughly satisfied with all of the neat sounds I was making. Of all the items back there though, the aluminum ladder was the best. It gave a very satisfying ring. I started at one end and made my way to the other rapping in between and on each rung; I was especially pleased when I could hear the pitch change slightly as I went along. Glee only partially describes the feeling I had. The ladder was lying on its side and I knelt down to get a good shot at the other side of the ladder that was on the floor. I then proceeded to make my way down that side of the ladder. I went along as before banging on each rung, and then there it was.

I had never seen anything quite like this. It was quite odd. It was semi-conical shaped and hanging on the ladder itself. It was only a couple of inches wide, and looked like old brown paper. The oddest thing about it was all of these funny looking bugs crawling on it. I sat, just inches from it, for a couple of minutes just watching these yellow and black bugs with wings walk around on it, and fly here and there. That was probably the oddest thing to me, the way they just walked around and buzzed, but never really went very far. Then I became curious about how it would sound, so I hit it with the hammer. That was very disappointing; it didn't make any noise at all. However, it sure seemed to excite those funny yellow and black bugs. Then I discovered just how excited they were.

A Hammer and a Four-Year-Old

I don't know exactly how many times I got stung before I got to Granny, but I do remember that at least one of them got me on the nose. The intense fire I felt at their sting was unlike anything I had ever experienced, and these bugs were all over me. I was terrified. I ran and ran, and cried out for Granny to help me. I was frantic.

Finally, I reached the top of the stairs on the back porch and Granny was there waiting for me. She grabbed me up and rushed me inside, quickly closing the door behind us. She gently held me and kissed my teary face, assuring me that I would be ok. She then explained to me that those were yellow jackets and that I had been stung. I still wasn't quite sure what it meant to be stung, but I knew that I did not want to do it again.

The other thing I discovered in this grand adventure is the fact that grandparents have odd ways of remedying common issues and ailments. Granny then took her tea bag from her teacup she had been drinking from and had me hold it on my nose. I thought that she was crazy, but hey, she's Granny, I'll go with it. I don't know if the tea bag actually did anything, but after a while I felt much better. Before I went out again to ride my painted horse, we both agreed that perhaps the hammer was not the best thing for me to have, and I definitely needed to give my new friends the yellow jackets a wide berth.

A Balanced Meal

On this mountain the Lord of hosts will make for all peoples a feast of rich food, a
feast of well-aged wines, of rich food filled with marrow, of well-aged wines
strained clear.

Isaiah 25:6

Grandpa was one of those guys who truly knew what it meant to suck the marrow from the bone of life; he and my grandmother lived their lives to the fullest. All that God placed here they enjoyed and relished. It did not matter if it was a hug from his granddaughter or a handful of freshly tilled earth, he enjoyed it for all it had to offer.

Food was always an integral part of life in their home. Food permeated every aspect of life there. They were involved in growing, tending, harvesting, canning, preserving, preparing, and most especially, eating. In their house it was quite the symbiotic relationship; Grandpa grew it, Grandma prepared it, and Grandpa ate it.

They both loved food, the mystique of the way family would gather around in all aspects of it, and savoring its goodness. Grandma constantly came up with new recipes that had to be tried. She would get Grandpa to grow things that should never have been able to be grown in the area where they lived, but they grew it consistently with glowing success. During the months that it would grow, Grandpa would tend it and spoil it like a beloved grandson.

Grandpa would tend to each phase of the new plants life with nothing short of tenderness and love. Usually, he started in the late fall and early winter by gathering seeds for it from that year's harvest. Then he would plant them in sets in the house; daily making sure they had sufficient water and light. He put tremendous effort into ensuring that he used the proper blend and proportions of fertilizer. He watched the little sprout as it began to break through the soil with tremendous glee, and inevitably would escort my siblings and me to go witness the new life breaking forth on our next visit with him.

When spring would finally arrive, Grandpa would take the now healthy plant sets out and plant them in the garden. Again, he would take great care to protect them and feed them. Each would be properly supported, staked, guarded, or whatever was needed; no aspect was overlooked. When it began to grow to its full height, he was there every day with the pruning shears and the twine. As it grew the branches that would sap energy from the plant without producing fruit were removed, and the ones that were fruitful were supported. He would continue to water and fertilize each plant individually and make sure that it was well-supported with plenty of dirt piled around its base.

When the harvest came, Grandpa was there. Each day he would collect the fruits of his labors. Each tomato, green bean, ear of corn, turnip, or stalk of rhubarb was inspected. If it did not pass his scrutiny it was thrown into the compost bin to help feed the plants that were still producing. If it did pass his watchful eye, then it was delivered to Grandma to prepare something truly delightful.

One of Grandma's particular specialties was sauerkraut; it was divine. Made from cabbage from their garden, the two of them would carefully wash and prepare the cabbage. She would prepare her special pickling brine and put the combination in ceramic crocks where they would be left to become a true delight. Even most of the herbs for the brine were grown in their garden.

Sometime after the kraut was ready we would gather for a meal of German specialties; usually some kind of sausage, potato salad, and their kraut. Very few items found on the table did not come from their garden. Each of us would eat well beyond the sin of gluttony just trying to keep pace with Grandpa, and never really succeeding. Then, just when we thought that we could not possibly eat any more, Grandma would announce that desert was ready.

Often she would prepare a cake (homemade of course), with icing that would melt in your mouth. She would usually have some ice cream to go with it. Grandpa was always health conscious and took great pains to point out to my sister, brother, and I that our diets should at all times be balanced. Our meals should always include vegetables, protein, dairy, and fruit. Beyond that, desert as well should be balanced; never should you allow your cake to outweigh your ice cream.

Grandpa's philosophy in the art of eating and enjoying desert would be that if your dessert experienced an imbalance then you should adjust the proportions to bring it back to a state of homeostasis. So, if the relationship between ice cream and cake were not according to that delicate balance where cake outweighs ice cream, then you should add more ice cream to your dish until they balanced. If it became unbalanced in the other direction, then you should add cake to balance it out; removing one of the items was never an option. Grandpa would repeat this process until either the cake or the ice cream (or most frequently – both) was gone. This was Grandpa's variation on Zen and the Art of Eating Desert.

My siblings and I discovered, unfortunately, that our parents did not share the same philosophy as Grandpa. We would use the same arguments that he used and they would fall on deaf ears. Wiping out an entire cake or container of ice cream in order to keep our dietary chi in balance was neither encouraged nor allowed, but it never really stopped us from trying or savoring the fullness of whatever we did have to enjoy with Grandpa's enthusiasm.

Grandpa was a man that loved his food and his family. All of us felt his loving touch. He would help support each of us in any endeavor, carefully getting us started. He would keep us going with regular encouragement. He carefully pruned us if we sprouted of in the wrong direction. And, he proudly brought us in and presented us when he felt that we had met the mark. He then continued to love us until there was nothing left. Grandma simply had a way of turning bitter rhubarb into the sweetest of pies. It did not matter how bitter we were, under her sugary touch we became as sweet as honey.

Tobacco Road

How very good and pleasant it is when kindred live together in unity! It is like the precious oil on the head, running down upon the beard, on the beard of Aaron, running down over the collar of his robes.

Psalm 133:1-2

One memory that I have of Papaw, which most of my cousins do not have is him smoking; he was a product of his generation. I remember him smoking filterless Camel cigarettes; that was, of course, after he no longer rolled his own cigarettes. He would sit in his chair in the den and smoke those cigarettes, read Zane Grey or Louis L'Amour novels, and be as content as he could be (I would venture that most of my cousins also do not remember him reading Zane Grey novels either). However, in 1965, when the surgeon general, Luther Terry, mandated the legislation that eventually added the surgeon general's warning on all smoking products, the face of smoking in the US changed drastically.

Before he quit smoking, the sounds emanating from him every morning were horrifying. The long sessions of hacking and coughing, and expelling the poisons from his lungs in great wads of phlegm were pretty much enough to convince me long before I had ever heard of a surgeon general that smoking was probably a bad idea. That image of him was the best anti-smoking ad that I ever saw.

It was another couple of years for Papaw to quit smoking, but, from my perspective, it was virtually an overnight change. No whining. No great struggle. No debate. Simply done. Gone was the pedestal ashtray next to his chair. Gone were the cartons of cigarettes in the cabinet. All that remained were a few empty tobacco tins, and some rolling papers from the days that he rolled his own before he graduated to Camel filterless, and over the next few years those disappeared as the cabinets were cleaned out from time to time. Now as altruistic as you may think his divorcing himself from cigarettes may be, he did pick up another vice which stuck with him to his dying day and beyond, chewing tobacco.

His first foray into chewing tobacco began with plugs of tobacco, a hard brick of tobacco from which he would cut off a piece to chew.

That was relatively short lived until he discovered Red Man loose leaf chewing tobacco, which he would just take a big pinch of it out of the pouch and put it in his mouth to chew. No matter the source, however, what did remain constant from that time forward were brown dribbles down his chin and an Astor frozen concentrate orange juice can for a spittoon continuously in his hand.

I am not sure if cigarettes in his life provided as much color to the way that he lived his life before he stopped smoking as chewing tobacco did after he started to chew, but I can't imagine what that would have looked like if it had been as colorful. Between the tobacco, the cans, and unusual circumstances it just goes on and on with chewing tobacco.

Normally, as we were just walking around a spittoon was not necessary; he just spit on the ground. However, driving, sitting around in the house, or other functions did require the spittoon. I suspect Mamaw is thankful that he did not see the need to buy an expensive spittoon, and chose instead to reuse a product around the house. An Astor frozen concentrate orange juice can is unique and well-suited, as much as anything is. Because it was designed to hold a frozen liquid it doesn't leak. Because it is heavy cardboard with a tin bottom you don't have to see what is coming back out of Papaw's mouth. The top opening being nice and wide is both good and bad. It is good because it gives him a big target to aim for. It is bad because it is easily spilled.

There is no doubt that I am in good company with the vast majority of my cousins in having been instructed to hold his can for him from time to time. Inevitably, we would be driving somewhere and Papaw would turn to me and say, "Here boy, hold this can for me;" this was not my idea of a good time. A typical can would last him a month or more, and let me tell you there is a lot of nastiness on the outside of his cans in that month. If I resisted, which I often did, I got in return, "Boy, just hush and hold that thing while I drive, it ain't gonna' bite ya'."

If we were out somewhere he would normally want to bring his can with him. Mamaw was quite good at helping him to draw some appropriate boundaries for where to take his can, and where not to. For instance, going into church was probably not a great place to take the can. Going into a fancy restaurant also fell into that category.

But, just because he did not take his can does not also imply that he did not take his chewing tobacco.

When my cousin, Laura, got married the family gathered in an absolutely spectacular restaurant on the St John's River in Jacksonville, FL. The view, the food, and the company were beyond compare. Family had traveled both near and far to celebrate this great occasion. While at dinner Papaw indicated that he needed to visit the restroom, and with a little help he made his way there. One of my cousins was in charge of making sure that he made it to and from the restroom without incident. While taking care of his business in the restroom, however, he slipped in a wad of tobacco to chew on, but did not have his requisite spittoon / Astor orange juice can with him. The restaurant was one of those fancy seafood restaurants with plenty of brass accessories around as decorations, and Papaw spotted one that looked a lot like a spittoon to him. Seizing the opportunity, he used the "spittoon" that he found, just as my cousin was trying to stop him. Unfortunately, he did not stop him in time from spitting into a very nicely polished brass ship's compass. Papaw was amused by his own mistake, but did not like the idea of having to get rid of his tobacco; he had just put it in. So, being the frugal man that he was, he pulled out the wad and put it back into his Red Man pouch to be used later that evening; again, recycle and reuse.

Papaw approached going to church or other events in much the same way. He agreed to leave his can in the car or truck, but he would still chew tobacco right up until the last possible minute. At church he would hold court with several other men from the church who also were chewing, or smoking, or maybe just swearing too much to go directly into church on a patio near the church entrance. Mamaw would go into the church and find their regular pew and get settled in. As the prelude would begin she would come out and tell him, "Philip, get in this church right now, church is beginning."

Papaw took that as a sign to get his last few chews in and exchange at least one more story about his new heifer. As the prelude came to an end Mamaw would stick her head out the church door again, a bit more insistent this time, "Philip, I mean it. You spit that tobacco out right now and get in here; the preachin' is about to begin." He would then reluctantly pull out the mighty wad of tobacco from his mouth and return it to his tobacco pouch for later use. As the church service came to a close he would beat a hasty exit, beating the pastor to the door as the postlude began, and before he hit the bottom step outside the church the wad of tobacco he saved earlier was returned to his mouth. He was in good company since the gentlemen he had been speaking with prior to church were already there with him.

As frugal as he was about his tobacco, I guess I have to say that I am honored that he considered using some of his precious product for my needs. Several times while visiting with my grandparents I would be invited by a friend of the family to go fishing. Frugality ran deep and wide throughout that community and there would be no stopping at the bait and tackle store to buy any store-bought worms. No sir; I dug my own worms.

The area next to the barn was some of the muddiest area on the planet, but also one of the greatest for finding worms. For one of these fishing expeditions while I was digging up some worms and putting them in a container to take with me, my spade got a lot of mud caked on it. I took the spade and smacked it against the side of the barn to knock off the mud, which worked relatively well. However, it also worked well to agitate the hornets in the nest directly above my head that I had not seen, and several of them approached me to more fully express their displeasure in me disrupting their nest.

I happily and eagerly would have run, but the mud was so squishy that it was about halfway up my calves and I wasn't going anywhere in a hurry. Fortunately, and with a lot of effort, I did break free, but not before I ended up with several stings for my troubles.

Nearby, Papaw saw the whole thing happen, and once he was able to stop laughing about how ungainly I was stuck in mud and swatting at hornets he was able to express some sympathy for my plight. Out of a sense of deep compassion and love, I am sure, he offered me a solution. "Here boy," as he pulled the wad of tobacco from his mouth, "put this on it. It'll pull that sting right out of it."

"What?!?" I looked back at him incredulously as he extended out his arm with the mighty, dripping, spit-covered wad in his hand to me. "Papaw, that's nasty. I don't want to put that on me."

"Now boy, just do what I say!" as he shoved the warm, brown mush into my hand. "Here now, put that on it."

Reluctantly, I did. And, to my amazement, within a couple of minutes the pain was effectively gone. Of course, I did not want to admit that to him, but it did work. And, even more importantly, I was still able to go fishing.

Papaw's love for his tobacco was known throughout the community, to friends and family near and wide. Tommy, a local neighbor, also raised cattle, and in Papaw's last few years leased the land for his own cattle from Papaw. They really did have a special and tender friendship that I could tell meant a lot to both of them. I think Tommy saw in Papaw much of what I had my entire life, and I had loved the fact that someone else appreciated him the way that I did.

Besides raising cattle and running a farm, Tommy was also one of the local funeral directors, and it was a tremendous honor for him to help prepare Papaw's body for burial. He made sure that he had the right suit on, his glasses, and the things that made him look like my grandfather should have looked. However, Tommy took great glee in sharing with me that he had also put a pouch of Red Man in Papaw's jacket pocket, "for the journey." Of course, I forgot to ask Tommy about the Astor orange juice can because Mamaw would not put up with him spitting in that coffin.

Cider with Mr. Jim

Give strong drink to one who is perishing, and wine to those in bitter distress; let
   them drink and forget their poverty, and remember their misery no more.

Proverbs 31:6-7

Each summer during most of my teen years I would spend with
Mamaw and Papaw. Each day, Papaw and I would conquer different
tasks and visit friends around the community. To me, there seemed to
be no real rhyme or reason as to what we would do or where we
would go, and oddly enough I never questioned this. Usually, when
Papaw and I would pile into the truck I had no clue as to where we
were going, what we were doing, or whom we were going to see. I
just knew that he told me to climb into the truck and I did. However,
one of our usual stops that was a true treat was Mr. Jim's.

Mr. Jim was a unique old man who lived just a short walk from
Mamaw and Papaw's house. He never lived by any pretense. His life
and his lifestyle were untainted by the world around him, and it was
dead simple.

Mr. Jim was about 15 years Papaw's senior. His house was a
simple slat board style house with a tin roof. Neither running water,
nor electricity had ever passed through its portals. It is also unlikely
that a bucket of paint had ever seen that house either. Each board
creaked of a simple, no frills life. The only modern convenience he
had was a simple battery operated radio and a windup alarm clock,
and that's all he wanted.

The old house stood under an old oak tree that provided shade for
the front porch, which is where you would normally find Mr. Jim
sitting. Mr. Jim took scruffy to a whole new level. I never saw him
wear anything but an old pair of blue jeans style coveralls. He would
sit up on that old porch in a ladder back chair with his skinny legs
crossed and leaning on one knee as he eyed you across the yard. He
only had a few sprigs of hair coming from his relatively shiny head,
and rarely shaved either. I am confident that Mr. Jim had bathed
before in his life, but he was certainly not going to wear out his wash
basin any time soon.

Behind the house stood a orchard of apple trees. None very fancy or finely pruned, just growing as God had intended; kind of scraggly just like Mr. Jim. Continuing on beyond the house, beside the apple orchard was Mr. Jim's outhouse – his version of modern plumbing. The other half of his modern plumbing was a freshwater spring that provided his drinking water.

To get to the spring, you would continue down the hill, beyond Mr. Jim's house, on the other side of the apple orchard. It was the type of path that fairy tale legends are made of. Well grown, lush and green with a mossy carpet of grass and undergrowth lining the path. The canopy of trees formed a tunnel through the woods that permitted only the slightest amount of light in. In the heat of summer at high noon you were cool and almost tempted to take a flashlight. The path meandered through the woods for about a half a mile. When you reached the bottom of the hill, you also reached the spring. Sunk into the ground where the spring was formed was a piece of cement sewer pipe up on its end. This allowed a pool to form about a foot and a half deep with a river rock bottom, which helped keep dirt and silt from the water. The water from this spring was sweet and cold. Just on the other side of the spring, Mr. Jim had placed an old wooden mailbox that perpetually had moss growing on it with an old metal dipper. These had the appearance of having been there forever, which they may have been. But, I always took a large ladle full of water and enjoyed its cold refreshing taste on a hot summer day.

Mamaw and Papaw collected their gallon milk jugs for Mr. Jim, and about once a week we would carry the cleaned empty jugs to him. Papaw would then send me down to the spring to collect water for Mr. Jim. This was a special treat for me since I would get to use the dipper to get a little for myself. I would carry the two one-gallon jugs down and fill them up. While I was down there I would try to find crawdads and get many ladles full of water before returning back up the hill. I was especially amazed at how much heavier those jugs became once filled with water. Mr. Jim was about 90 at this time and getting up and down that hill was not easy for him, so this simple act was visibly appreciated by him, and a pleasure for me to do.

One summer that I spent with Papaw, as usual, he told me to get into the truck early in the morning with him. We pulled around behind the house and filled the bed with apples that had fallen from the tree behind the car shed. Then we went up the road to Mr. Inman's house and got all of his apples off the ground. Then with Mr. Inman in tow, we headed down to see Mr. Jim. I still didn't really know what we were going to do.

When we arrived Mr. Jim was sitting on his porch as usual, with his usual inviting smile that included a couple of his original teeth. He may have owned other clothes, but I never saw him in anything but blue denim coveralls. Mr. Jim and Papaw proceeded across the yard to an old wooden device sitting in the yard under the large oak tree. It was covered by a galvanized tin bucket upside down. When they pulled off the bucket it revealed a machine that I had never seen before; they called it a cider press.

The cider press was formed with a main supporting framework of solid 4x4 beams. The framework was about 3 feet high by 4 feet long and 2 feet wide. Going along the bottom was sluice made from planks about ½" thick that had a slight slope to it going along the framework lengthwise. At one end of the framework was a chute made from the same ½" thick wood that led into a chamber made from the same material. That chamber exited out above the sluice. Inside the chamber was a barrel shaped drum with metal teeth on its outer perimeter. The drum was connected to a shaft that came out one side to a hand crank and the other side to a flywheel. At the opposite end of the framework was a large metal screw with a double handle crank at the top. The screw went down from the top of the framework toward the sluice. On the lower end of the screw was a wooden disk made from multiple layers of wood about 1 ½" thick. Riding on top of the sluice was an odd looking wooden bucket. There were slats in the bucket each only about 1" wide and separated from the next slat by about 1".

Mr. Jim put a piece of cheesecloth in the bucket that was on the sluice and lapped it over the edges. Then Papaw and Mr. Jim told me to start turning the hand crank going to barrel inside of the chamber. At this point, Mr. Inman, Mr. Jim, and Papaw began to throw apples into the chute at the top. It was much more difficult to get the drum turning than I thought it would be. It must have taken me about a minute to get it up to speed, but I stuck with it. None of the three men even thought of offering to help because they knew that I was more than capable and had way too much pride to let one of them do it. However, Mr. Jim did help in his own very unique way; he sang.

"Me and my wife and stump tailed dog, crossed the creek on an old oak log…" If I wasn't already in the country, I just got sent very deep into old country. As long as I turned that wheel he sang that old song. Actually, to describe it as singing is probably being a bit generous since I doubt that he used more than about two notes and those weren't on pitch, but I loved it and I would do just about anything to hear that again today. As I have discovered this was his own version of "Little Brown Jug" without the identifiable tune or words; ah, but everyone is a music critic. It also fits with the mystique that defined Mr. Jim since it is a song primarily associated with moonshining.

As I turned the handle I was noticing that the apples they were throwing in the chute were not exactly the pick of the apples. In fact, most of them were somewhat rotten or worm infested. No apple was too good or too bad to be considered for making cider. The gap between the teeth on the outer rim of the barrel and the chute was very small, and really was too small for even an apple seed to make it through unscathed so the likelihood that a worm from one of the apples made it through in one piece was impossible (for those who may have enjoyed some of that cider with me over the years you probably don't really want to think very deeply about that part of the reality of cider making). As I turned the bucket under the chamber began to fill with apple pulp and the juice started to flow down the sluice where Mr. Jim had placed a clean, white, porcelain, enamel metal bucket to collect the juice.

After about ten minutes the bucket under the chute was full of apple pulp and Mr. Jim told me, "'at 'll do boy," which of course everyone understands that means, "We have ground a sufficient amount of apple pulp to move on with the next part of the process, so if you would be so kind as to stop the machine that would be wonderful."

Unfortunately, my Mr. Jim universal translator was not functioning at its optimum level so I responded in the only way I knew, as I huffed and puffed turning the hand crank, "What?"

Papaw then helped me out a bit and said, "Boy, go ahead and stop that thing."

"Oh, OK", and foolishly, I attempted to do just that. I stopped putting forward motion onto the hand crank and tried to stop it. What resulted from this action is one of my first studies into Newton's laws and I found that bodies in motion tended to stay in motion. Since the mechanical advantage caused by the flywheel far exceeded my own hold on the gravitational forces of the planet I became part of Newton's experiments and went into motion myself, and was launched headlong across the yard. Mr. Jim, Papaw, and Mr. Inman all three loved this and practically begged me to try it again. Fortunately, I was a quick study and decided that this was not in my best interest and certainly not the approach that I wanted to take in the future.

Once the barrel came to a stop on its own, Mr. Jim gently folded the flaps of the cheesecloth over into the bucket below. Then he slid it down until it was under the vertical screw mechanism. Then we started to turn the screw until it the wooden plate at the end of it started to press down onto the apple pulp under the cheesecloth. The more we turned this mechanism, the more juice came pouring from the sluice until we reached a point that we could no longer turn and no further juice was coming out anyway. Mr. Jim then took another metal ladle and tested the batch and declared through his toothless grin, "Ah, jus' right."

Eventually, I was given a ladle full of the cider. It was tangy and sweet at the same time. It was nothing like the apple juice that I had gotten at the store. Instead this was a darker brown cloudy liquid with much more tang to it. Mr. Jim was exactly right, it was absolutely fabulous, and I was hooked. It was probably the flavor added by the worms.

We made a few more passes worth of the cider that afternoon. We had enough that Mr. Inman was able to take some home with him and Papaw and I were able to take a couple of gallons home with us. Mr. Jim put his in a ceramic crock that sat out on his porch.

One thing I learned about real homemade cider is that it doesn't have a very long shelf life. After about a week you have apple cider vinegar and it is almost impossible to drink. Mr. Jim found that if he put about a cup of sugar in his and left it on his porch it became something much more entertaining. The sugar in the cider combined with the fact that Mr. Jim had no power and therefore no refrigeration which meant that the cider was constantly warm. This would cause his cider to start to go through a fermentation process. I tested some of his cider after just a few days, and I am positive that there are a number of states that his concoction would have been illegal in, and certainly illegal to have been serving to me.

Mr. Jim's simple life and ways were a tremendous blessing on me. Papaw was wise enough to see that the influence of that simple life would demonstrate to me that there is a certain magic to living beyond the cares of the world, and I will be eternally grateful for that lesson.

Gospel Music

Make a joyful noise to God, all the earth; sing the glory of his name; give to him glorious praise. Say to God, "How awesome are your deeds! Because of your great power, your enemies cringe before you. All the earth worships you; they sing praises to you, sing praises to your name."

Psalm 66:1-4

Papaw loved gospel music about as much as he loved his family. At one point in his life he would travel for hours to hear a gospel quartet. If he could have found a way to combine gospel music with a Braves game then he would have been in Heaven early. The odd thing was that Papaw knew nothing of making music himself. The ability to hold or carry a tune completely eluded him.

I remember once going to church with Papaw, which for some reason that Sunday was just the two of us. He and I had would stand during the hymns and he would tap his foot, but would never utter a word – not one. Naively I thought that Papaw simply did not have a hymnal available from which to read. I gave him a nudge with my elbow and put the hymnal where he could read from it. He gave me one of those looks that said, "What on earth are you thinking?" However, he began to sing. It was about that time that I got a very clear understanding of exactly why he normally was an observer and not a participant when it came to music. Fortunately it was a relatively short hymn, and the pain ended quickly enough for us all. He did hit a couple of different notes during the course of the hymn, but I don't think either of those notes were in the original score of the music. Mr. Ed, who usually sat near Papaw in the rear of the church, never fully grasped how far his version of a particular tune was from what was printed, and he didn't really care either. Mr. Ed, much to our chagrin, fully enjoyed making a joyful noise to the Lord; a loud and joyful noise. Despite the fact that he was musically disabled I am so thankful for his spirit and enthusiasm in singing with all his heart.

Papaw was always one to tell you exactly what he thought. He reminded me on more than one occasion that he was a National League man when I brought up any American League team, especially the Yankees. His stance was just as strong in politics. I would, on some occasions, bring up a republican in politics. In his eyes I could have just as easily brought up the devil himself. He was a democrat through and through, and was very proud of the fact that he always voted straight ticket. His thoughts on gospel music were no less exact. The group should always be a quartet, and should always have the traditional soprano, alto, tenor, and bass – although I am not fully convinced that he had a clue about the differences between the soprano and alto. As far as musical accompaniment goes, an upright piano was fine, but never should the music of the devil, found in a guitar, be found there. Bringing up the subject of drums was not a wise idea either. It was never very difficult to tell that even a tambourine was flirting with disaster to Papaw. His gospel music was pure vocal and piano – nothing more – nothing less.

He often took me with him to various gospel "sangin's". We would go to high school gyms, local churches, fire departments, or wherever the various quartets went that attracted Papaw. They were always well attended, and it seemed that my Papaw knew everyone there. It would take what seemed like hours just to find our way to our seats. The people we ran into always asked how he was and who this young man was with him. I loved my grandfather more than just about anything, and it was easy to see from the way he responded to his friends that he felt the same way about me. He would put his arm around me and rub his rough hand across my face. His tanned and leathery face would crack into a huge smile and he would proudly exclaim that, "this is Bobby's boy, John David. He wanted to come to the sangin' with me tonight."

The following litany was always the same, but I never tired of hearing it. Each person would always recount how many thousands of years that they had known Papaw. They would tell me how they used to play on the baseball team that he drove the bus for, or they helped him pick tobacco or cotton, or they lived on the farm adjacent to him, or any of any number of ways that Papaw was known throughout the region. However, always he seemed to be as much of a hero in their eyes as he was in mine.

Papaw and I would eventually make our way to our seats. The venues that these events were held in were never what you would consider posh; usually, it was building that everyone else had tired of using. The seats were always the metal folding kind. The piano was occasionally tuned, but rarely tuned well. But, there was more heart in that small space than could be contained in any room. The people were in love with Jesus and it was easy to tell. Each song would relate the story of the gospel in its own way. Through Papaw's rough exterior the music would tame his soul and the gospel it proclaimed would heal it. The music would start and he would quietly sit and pat his foot to the beat. He was never showy about it or made a big production about it. He just quietly sat, smiled, and patted his foot to the beat.

All too soon the sangin' would be over, and it would be time to find our way back to the pickup truck to go home. Mamaw would be waiting for us, and would ask how the sangin' was. Papaw would always say that it was just beautiful, but would rarely mention a single song that was sung. Instead, it was the people – he simply loved being with and around other people. He would list off each person, who they were with, how they were doing, and what visitation they needed to go to tomorrow; life for them always seemed to center around the next funeral to attend.

Going to a visitation is an important event in the south. After a person dies the funeral home will arrange for a visitation at the funeral home. Here the family of the deceased will gather, while the community "visits" with them and expresses their sympathy. In most other communities around the country this is referred to as a wake, but in Iredell County it is a visitation. In some ways, Mamaw and Papaw seemed to live for visitations. It is truly an odd existence in life to live as if you are anticipating and even looking forward to the next death. It makes you wonder if they were actually anticipating and looking forward to their own death.

Each morning we would gather in the kitchen around the table for a phenomenal home cooked breakfast. There is no doubt in my mind that this scrumptious breakfast did very little to lower a cholesterol level, but it sure was good. Mamaw and Papaw would listen to an old AM radio on top of the refrigerator to find out what the weather was to be like, and who had died so that they would know which visitations they needed to go to that night. However, often Papaw would hear of one at a sangin' that had not been announced on the radio yet, and this information was too important to let rest. Immediately, Mamaw and Papaw would make their plans around it.

For much of my memory in Papaw's life, he carried a simple Elgin pocket watch. It wasn't fancy or tremendously valuable. He seemed to be forever pulling it out of his pocket to wind it; seemed to be a continuous endeavor. Rarely did it feel like more than about thirty minutes would pass without Papaw pulling it out to check the time and wind it again. From my recollection, this was a constant fixture associated with my grandfather. After he died I was tremendously blessed when my family allowed me to have this watch. It represented more than just an heirloom to me; it is the constant reminder of a simple man, who loved the Lord and his family. It is in part, my inheritance.

I was proud of the way my family handled the remaining heirlooms that my grandparents left behind when they died. For some items it was like the proverbial white elephant that no one wants and others items there found a little competition. My grandfather's pocket watch was one of the items that found some competition, but there was no animosity or spitefulness by anyone for any item. We all gathered as a family and took turns selecting an item. My first round draft pick I took my grandfather's watch. However, one item that never was up for competition was his love of gospel music; I think in some ways the entire family inherited that.

As mentioned before, and it can't be overstated, Papaw's love of gospel music was only rivaled by his love of his family. Over the years he instilled in me that same love. It was slow and deliberate the way that he introduced me to both, but by the time he died I had it. His watch, though I love it, is only an heirloom. The watch is nothing more than a piece of fancy metal in the form of a watch that actually only keeps time in way that my grandfather kept time. Papaw always got there, but in his own time, in his own way, and with much love surrounding it; timeliness, however, was never part of the bargain. But my real inheritance is the one that cannot be put on the auction block or in a box. My real inheritance is the love that Papaw had for gospel music, my family, and the Braves.

Work on the Farm

For we are God's servants, working together; you are God's field, God's building. According to the grace of God given to me, like a skilled master builder I laid a foundation, and someone else is building on it. Each builder must choose with care how to build on it.

1 Corinthians 3:9-10

Someone, who has never experienced putting in an actual day's work on a no-kidding working farm, would have trouble putting the experiences of farm life into a world view that they can fathom. I am not referring to the large industrial farms with a dozen hired hands; no this is a family farm where the family are the hired hands. In this kind of life there simply is not an excess amount of money to just go buy fancy new things to do basic tasks. You take what you have and come up with ways to build, repurpose, repair, or whatever. In short, you just figure it out. I once had a factory owner / manager tell me that he would rather hire either a farmer or a veteran because both knew how to just get things done with what they have. His maintenance manager was both; prior service Marine and a farmer, and that factory owner could not have been happier.

I discovered early on that I have somewhat of an aptitude for being able to just figure things out. My time in the Navy was helped out by my experiences on the farm, and also amplified that technical capability in a very helpful way.

As a farmer and rancher Papaw maintained a herd of beef cattle for most of my memory with him. I do have some memory, early on, of the dairy cattle he raised, but those went away when his primary milking machine graduated high school and went to Appalachian State University. Neither he nor my grandmother was very interested in the laborious task of milking the cows every day once they were the ones responsible for it every day. In beef cattle your money is made when you successfully raise and sell one of your herd to market, and, for the most part, beef cows are pretty good about eating.

Papaw would often just sell his cows outright to be processed, but other times he would work a bargain where he got part of the processed meat in payment. It is no trivial thing to fill your freezer with beef to feed your family for months, and it would cost him much less than going to the local grocery store to buy all that meat. However, getting a cow to market is no small feat either.

Cows don't do stairs or steps up very enthusiastically, and they definitely do not appreciate going down steps at all. As a result, you have two options – you can either use a ramp of some kind or you can position your hauling vehicle in such a way that the cow simply steps from dirt directly into the vehicle. Since it is tricky to find a place you can back your truck or trailer up to that has just the right hill, most farmers build or use ramps. Papaw fell in the latter category and built his own ramp.

Papaw's ramp was about 20 feet long and came up to exactly the height of his tailgate for his pickup truck. He built the form from old lumber and boards from around the farm, and then the only real purchase was the cement for the ramp itself. It was well-made and ingenious. It really did work perfectly to guide a cow to the back of the awaiting pickup truck. Of course, it took a lot of convincing to encourage the cow to make that walk up the ramp; they usually had other ideas of what they wanted to be doing. Perhaps the cows were aware of what awaited them at the other end of that truck ride.

Looking at that ramp you get a great idea of how rustic things can look and still be functional. The fence rails and posts forming the sides are not refined. The posts are lengths of cedar trees from around the farm that were cut down, cut to length, and the limbs trimmed off. Manual posthole diggers were used to place the poles. The sides are rough cut planks, with heavy emphasis on the "rough cut" portion. Your average 84-Lumber would not even sell these as seconds or off-quality; they don't meet even that standard. The poured cement is really more like a bunch of bags of Sakrete roughly mixed and poured in to form the ramp; it is neither smooth, nor refined. In short, this ramp will never win a beauty contest, but it works and it works well.

Periodically, fence lines needs to be changed, removed, or repaired. Once Papaw wanted to pull the barbed-wire fence up from around a field that had not held cattle in probably a decade or more; he never really gets in a hurry to make these kinds of changes. However, we had to start with making a reel to coil up the old barbed-wire.

There is no doubt in my mind that we could have easily gone down to Beaver's Country Store or any number of hardware stores and purchased a reel to coil this wire up on, but that was never going to happen. We had too much in the way of raw materials and way too much time on our hands to be spending money to do anything.

Without telling me what we were doing, Papaw had me cut 4 pieces of 1"x4" lumber into lengths of about 24". Then he had me cut 4 pieces of 1"x1" about the same length. Of course, those cuts were made with a hand saw, and, of course, it took a while. By the time I got to the last cut I pretty much had it down, but the first couple were a bit rough and certainly not the definition of straight.

His desire to have certain boards at certain lengths bears a little description. In the event that you think he may have actually used a ruler or tape measure or any other method of accurately determining length you would be sadly mistaken. In reality he used the width of fingers and hands and feet. It was not what I was expecting, but farm methods, as previously mentioned, are simple methods.

We also didn't have a workbench readily available that I could use to place the wood on to cut it. Instead, my "workbench" was the platform on which he stored the mowing machine that he would tow behind his tractor to make hay with. Of course, he did not tell me this at first and instead simply watched me flounder around for a while wrestling with a board and a saw in the dirt. Eventually, however, he came over and placed the board on the platform, then put his foot on it and showed me how to start a cut. Gently, with his leathery hands, he reached down to the board being cut to guide the saw blade to where he wanted the cut to go, just resting the blade against his thumb. Then he pulled back on the handle and allowed the saw blade to make a shallow bite into the wood from its own weight alone. After two or three pulls a small channel began to form that held the blade in place, and then he pushed and pulled with vigor and quickly severed the board at the perfect length. The end was perfectly straight and the length was spot on. "Now you do it," he encouraged me.

It took a couple of attempts to get my body to comply with stepping on the board on the platform without toppling over; this was a source of significant hilarity for him as he watched me. I then tried to just start pushing the saw right away, like a "real man," without getting it started first – this did not go well. It bounced and jostled all over the place. Ah, I had forgotten to guide it with my hand. So I got my hand in the mix to guide it, but still tried to muscle my way through. Again, it bounced and I discovered in a painful way why they refer to the cutting edge of the saw blade as "teeth". Those teeth are quite sharp and they can also do to human flesh about the same thing they can do to wood; lesson learned. Papaw was amused but not very sympathetic; he gave me an old rag to wrap around my hand while I finished the job. Finally, I stopped trying to muscle my way through and allowed the tool to do its job, and the cut started near perfectly. It felt spectacular as the bits of sawdust scattered from the point where the blade met wood. It was a tremendous feeling of accomplishment as I watched that first board fall to the dry, dusty ground with a satisfying thump. Of course, the nice straight and accurate lines he was able to produce did not quite match what I provided, but mine were just as functional.

As I finished making the remaining cuts my accuracy and efficiency improved. By the time I finished making the last cut I was pretty well spent and ready to call it a day, but little did I know that I was just getting started. Did I mention how much hard work goes into the running of a farm?

When I thought that I was done, he had me gather up the four pieces of 1"x4" that I had cut and find the center of them. He then instructed me to drill a 1 ½" hole at the center point. This was not to be done with a drill press, or a fancy electric drill; no, I was going to use a brace and bit. Although it was still amusing to watch, it went a bit smoother than my first cuts had gone; I had at least seen a brace and bit used before and had some comfort level with it. Also, Papaw was pretty good about keeping his bits sharp and in good shape. Of course, the bigger adventure was simply finding said brace and bit.

Tools at Papaw's were everywhere. He was never one of those anal retentive types who have a designated peg for every tool, and an outline around it like the police draw around dead bodies. He had somewhat of a system of where the tools were kept, but it was a bit fuzzy to just about everyone; sometimes even including him.

Besides the house itself there were four other, very rustic buildings that dotted the area around the house. Each of these buildings had multiple functions and multiple names, and these names were more of tradition than the reality of their current use. For instance, the first building you come to as you leave the main road is three buildings in one – the car shed, the granary, and the smoke house. The car shed actually did hold the car, but the granary did not hold grain and the only smoking that may have ever occurred in the smokehouse is Papaw with one of his filterless Camels when he still smoked. The granary held potatoes by the hundreds scattered on the floor and covered with sevindust, and the smoke house was filled with lawn equipment with onions hanging from the ceiling.

The barn was a straightforward barn. The floor was a continuous state of muddiness. The loft was filled with hay put up in the summer to be fed in the winter. Little alcoves existed where some cows would get in out of the weather. On each end of the barn was a tremendous door with a gate to control the flow of cattle, especially when we were preparing to send a cow to market.

The milk house had, at one point in its incarnation, been a milk house, and although it had ceased to function in that capacity many years before the name never went away. Instead it became a storage location for many of Papaw's tools, but also various bins of nuts, bolts, washers, screws, and many items that no one has a clue what they were for any longer. This was, of course, a great place to search for the brace and bit we were looking for, but we did not find it there.

The final of the four buildings is one of the largest, the tractor shed, but also called the tool shed. It did, in fact, house both the tractor and a multitude of tools, but it housed so much more. The truck was usually housed there, along with at least one neighbor's boat and the golf cart. It also contained the mowing machine, the hail bailer, the manure spreader, and various plows. It was an immense building, completely open on two sides with a tin roof. To be as open as it was, it still amazes me how dry the dusty floor always was. Even with the occasional torrential downpour the floor seemed to always be very dry and dusty.

The various hand tools, including the brace and bit we were looking for, were all in various shelves along one wall of the massive building. They were in no particular order, and there was no telling how much stuff was piled on top of whatever you were looking for. Fortunately for us, however, on this occasion we found the brace and bit with relative ease.

With the wood cut, and the holes drilled Papaw then instructed me on assembling our little project. As of this point, however, he was yet to tell me what we were making or what it would be used for. The odd thing was, I never really thought to ask either. Armed with hammer and nails we began to assemble our project. I nailed two of the 1"x4"s together in a cross pattern with the holes overlapping each other then did the same for the other two. Then, he had me nail the remaining 1"x1" pieces to connect the two crosses I had just constructed. What we ended up with is a reel or spool to put our barbed-wire on. I don't think that I could have ever envisioned the end product from the various pieces he had me prepare, but looking back on it, it makes perfect sense now.

We mounted the finished reel to the front of the tractor by passing a metal pipe through the center as an axle and connecting that pipe to channel beams that extended from the front of the tractor on which you mount various pieces farm machinery. I was impressed with our country ingenuity. I was excited to try to figure out to do all kinds of things from the nothing lying around us, but we still needed to get up that barbed-wire from the field.

We both climbed up onto the tractor and headed out to the field in question. From one end to the other was probably about a mile, and although the entire field did not have barbed-wire, most of it did. I walked in front of the tractor, continuously guiding the barbed-wire onto the reel and turning the reel by hand to gather up our fence line; this was a very long and laborious process. Papaw was not always the most attentive nor was he the best at being patient for me to move out of the way before he moved the tractor and there were a few times that I nearly became one with the soil under the tires of the tractor. Yet somehow we figured it out and got the job done without having to prepare my obituary. In the end we needed to make several more reels and spend many hours in the field gathering the barbed-wire, but we made it happen.

The barbed-wire fence that he and I reeled in was to be used to repair the fence in other places or rearrange the fence boundaries depending on his needs at that moment, but it was certainly not to be just thrown out. On the back side of Papaw's property, over near Charles' farm there was some fence line in need of repair. So, the next day, using our newly acquired barbed-wire we set out to do just that.

Papaw's farm was never pretentious or very large in comparison to some neighbor's farms. Papaw's was rolling farmland, green and lush. It was very good for cattle to wander around on, but as far as growing crops most of it would be challenging because of the uneven terrain and the multitude of trees. To this day I am thankful that going to a more industrial environment of a farm was never an incentive for my grandparents. I believe that would have just taken away from the joy of being one with that incredible piece of land.

Occasionally, an overzealous cow would knock down a section of fence, but with all the trees that are on the land, inevitably they will fall and take out sections of fence; that was the case near Charles' farm. Papaw and I loaded up various tools on the tractor and one of those reels of barbed-wire and headed out. It probably took us 30 minutes to make the journey because we, of course, had to stop and pick up nearly every stick we saw and toss it into the gulley. We also had to survey the various cows and just admire them for a while, especially the new white-face calf. However, eventually we did make it to our appointed destination.

We took the saws and axes we brought, and cut the fallen tree off the fence. Actually, more to the point, I cut it off with a LOT of direction and supervision from Papaw about how to and how not to cut. He was also generous enough to provide me with guidance about how slowly I was cutting through the tree; I am sure I would have never figured that out without his insight.

As we got to work on repairing the fence, though, Papaw pointed out to me that the other fence I was standing next to was Charles' and it was an electric fence. I had already bumped into several times unintentionally, and automatically assumed that it must not be on. Interesting thing about electric fences, they pulse. Electric fences do not put out continuous current; instead they provide periodic pulses of sufficient voltage to convince a cow that going further is a bad idea. These are facts that I was not aware of at the time so I told him, "No, it must be off," as I placed my bare hand on the wire to prove to him that it was off – for about a second, which at that time was about a second too long.

Work on the Farm

You know, once that voltage cycled on again during that moment that I held the wire I had a lot to think about. At the top of that list was my foolishness combined with searing pain radiating down my arm to the rest of my body. I let go of that wire as fast as my body would allow, yelling and screaming something terrible.

Between the commotion I created and the hysterics of laughter that Papaw fell into from watching me, our neighbor, Charles, took note of the fact that we were there and came over to see if we were OK. Papaw related to Charles the comedy of errors that I embodied to the point that both of them were nearly in tears. Of course, both of them had sympathy on me and shared about how they had done exactly the same thing, on more than one occasion. I guess that made me feel a little better, but only marginally and not any less stupid.

While we continued to work, Charles and Papaw talked about Charles' chickens and invited us over to help feed them later. They worked out the details while I hammered away on getting the barbed-wire back up, and the next day we paid a visit over to Charles' farm.

Up to this point in my life I had been around a lot of cattle, a few horses, an occasional pig, and very seldom a chicken of any kind. I was not quite prepared for what we walked into. In one of Charles' chicken coops was somewhere in the neighborhood of 600 chickens at various stages of development. This was industrial farming on a scale that I had only heard about but had never seen. The coop itself was divided into sections where the chickens were divided according to their stage of development. The section we went to in order to help Charles out they were probably a couple of months old.

Charles took me to the end of several conveyors that stretched out down the length of the section of the coop we were in. The conveyor was to deliver feed to the chickens on a schedule to help them grow. The only problem was, and always has been, chickens are stupid – that is why we were there and defined our job. Traditionally, farmers raising chickens would get a pail full of chicken feed and scatter it around on the ground near the chicken coop, but to feed this many chickens Charles would have had to have a pail about the size of a cement mixer. Since chickens are stupid and Charles did not have the time or a bucket the size of a cement mixer, we needed to help out.

It actually sounded pretty easy. All I needed to do was to shoo the chickens off the conveyor before it reached the end; otherwise, they would ride the conveyor to their peril. Really, no pressure here; if I screw my job up a bunch of chickens die. But, honestly, how hard can it be? Let me tell you, with chickens, it can be very hard.

Chickens discover very quickly that if they stand on the ground the feed goes past them, but if they stand on the conveyor belt that they travel with their food they don't have to keep chasing it. OK, so maybe they are not quite as stupid as we would like to think they are; they just aren't forward thinking and safety conscious.

As Charles fired up the conveyor and started the feed flowing onto it the chickens responded like Pavlov's dogs, ravenously. At first, it was no big deal at all as I positioned myself near the end of a couple of the conveyors and Papaw did the same between a couple more.

Shortly after the conveyor started, however, the chickens got quite a bit more enthusiastic about the food and they started staying on the conveyor even more. Eventually, I was beginning to feel like the episode of *I Love Lucy* where Lucy and Ethel are working in a candy factory and supposedly packaging the candy as it passes by on a conveyor; at first they did pretty well as well. Before long, though, just like Lucy and Ethel, I missed a couple and it really went poorly for the chickens.

Missing a few chickens was devastating to me, but that wasn't near as bad as Charles calmly coming by and dispassionately dispatching them to meet the Great Colonel Sanders in the sky a little earlier than anticipated because the end of the conveyor did not completely finish them off. His calmness in that act, I have to admit, kind of freaked me out a little, so I redoubled my efforts to save just a few more. Papaw missed a few too, but he was just as happy to dispatch the ones that slipped by as Charles was; it didn't seem to faze him in the least.

Death and disease are as real as part of farming as anything else is, but nothing quite prepares you for seeing it up close and personal like that. It is like the fact that we all have trash, but we don't really want to acknowledge it or even see it for that matter. As a matter of fact, trash is an important part of farm life because you can't just ignore it and hope it goes away. After all, even Arlo Guthrie discovered on Thanksgiving many years ago at Alice's Restaurant that you can neither ignore the trash nor handle it improperly, even though you can get anything you want there.

When winter arrives on a farm where there is an appreciable difference between summer and winter, the grass will all but cease to grow. Cows thrive on the grass they consume in the fields and when that grass disappears in the winter it can go very poorly for cows that are not fed daily from other sources. The hay that was stored in the barn was for just that purpose, but it certainly did not make its way to the cows on its own.

Whenever I came to their farm in the winter months I think Mamaw appreciated it more than just about anyone else. Of course I know she loved me, but she also loved the fact that she did not have to help Papaw feed the cows when I was there.

Papaw would back his old Chevy pickup truck to the barn near the opening to the hay loft and send me up into the hay loft. Up there I was to thrown down about 8 or 10 bales of hay into his truck where he was waiting to cut the bailing twine from it with his trusted and well-worn Barlow pocket knife. Once loaded, we headed out into the pasture; Papaw driving while I was in the back with the hay.

Fortunately, that old truck had sides on it that he had installed years before for the purpose of taking cows to market, although the rear doors were normally left off unless he was hauling a cow. The way that Papaw drove and the roughness of the pasture those sides are about the only reason that I did not topple over the side of the truck. The other trick depending on how recently he had hauled a cow, there may be a "gift" left by the cow on the floor of the truck; it is best to watch your step.

I clearly remember the day that Papaw, my father and uncles finished making those sides for his truck; I was maybe six or seven at the time. They were impressive additions to his truck, and another work of farm ingenuity. They were sturdy and well built. Assembling them on the truck was an amusing sight to watch.

I was clearly too young and small to try to get my little hands in the mix, but I was allowed to watch from a distance. They hoisted them up, and manhandled them one by one to fit them in place and put the interlocking pins in place that bound one side to another. At first, it looked great, but then they began to note that something was wrong; they couldn't see out of the truck's rear window. I came closer to the bunch of men and studied the conundrum with them and then pointed out, "You know, you've got it on upside down."

To a person they all laughed hysterically and slapped me on the back for noticing their faux pas. They then spent the better part of the next hour undoing what they had just done, and turning the whole thing over so that now you could carry a cow, and see.

One cold winter morning while everyone else was still enjoying a biscuit and cup of coffee, Papaw tugged on my shirt and said, "Come on boy." I didn't need to ask what for; I knew we were about to feed the cows.

As normal, we got the truck and backed it up under the window of the hayloft, and then Papaw sent me up to toss down bales of hay. I had grown some since last winter and now had the strength to easily pick up a bail and toss it on my own. The trick was not smacking Papaw in the head with a bail. Once loaded, we assumed our normal positions and headed out to the pasture.

One of my jobs was always to open and close the gate. I would jump down from the tailgate of the truck, run around and open the gate, let Papaw through, then run to close the gate and catch the truck; Papaw really wasn't one to wait around for me all day. So, I caught him and jumped up in the back of the pickup truck, carefully avoiding what the previous cow had left for me there.

Once we got out to the area he wanted to feed, Papaw would give me a shout and I would start feeding the hay a little at a time. For some reason, this particular day he seemed to be driving just a bit faster and a bit more rough than usual. Add on top of that the fact that I had probably grown an inch or so since last winter. At one point I was standing beneath the crossbar at the back end of the truck, which the previous year I had cleared easily. That year, however, it was a much tighter fit. When Papaw hit a bump it then launched me up, knocking the crown of my head into the pipe and sending me in a most spectacular manner sprawling amongst the cows I had just been feeding.

Knowing how much my grandfather loved me I was positive that he would immediately stop, and run back to see that I was OK. Nothing could have been further from the truth; he had no idea that I had been ejected from the truck so he continued on. I quickly gathered my senses and ran like mad to catch up to the truck, jumping in not long before he was ready for me to open the gate for him. I got to warm up with a pretty good bruise and an interesting story back in the house.

When you live on a farm, by definition, you are pretty remote because you just don't put farms in the middle of the city. Therefore, many of the city services that most people take for granted like water, sewer, trash, and similar services do not exists for farmers in the same way. In recent years some of these services have been extended further and further into the countryside, but most will never make their way out to the most remote farms and land.

Papaw's solution for trash was easy, burn it. He always kept a burn barrel on the edge of the garden and would burn the household trash almost every day. Any food scraps were either composted into the garden, fed to the cats and dogs, or fed to the cows. The ashes of the trash that was burned would then be composted into the garden. In many ways it was a very symbiotic system. The one weak link is the burn barrel.

Burn barrels are typically old 55 gallon drums that Papaw got from a wide variety of sources; it is probably best if we never ask where. After a number of uses, however, the metal would become thin and sitting out in the weather they would rust so each one had a very limited lifespan. Making a burn barrel last for a full year was considered a huge success. Most probably only lasted about 6-9 months, at best.

Depending on the barrel's configuration would determine what Papaw needed to do to prepare the barrel for use. Many have a lid that is clamped on using a strap; those are the simplest. Take the strap off, which releases the lid – done. The hard ones are where the lid is crimped onto the drum of the barrel. Those, the lid will need to be cut off in some manner. The one occasion that I remember witnessing and being asked to help, the barrel had a crimped on lid requiring it to be cut off. That is when the fun began.

Papaw pulled out a heavy chisel, or perhaps even a wedge like you split wood with, and handed it to me; picking the best tool for the job was not his forte. He then instructed me to hold the chisel on the top of the barrel near the edge. All of this seemed innocent enough so I complied, oblivious to what he was actually expecting of me. He then pulled out a 10 pound sledge hammer and reared back for a really big swing. It was not one of those swings where you are confirming distance. Nope, this was a swing that was meant to kill, devastate, and destroy. And I was holding the chisel with my bare hand.

At this point in his life Papaw was still pretty strong and virile; he was in his mid to late 70's and holding his own quite well. Despite that, and despite my tremendous love and trust for the man, there was no way on God's green earth that I was going to hold that chisel with my bare hand while he was taking a swing like that. What transpired next was truly comical.

As he came around in full swing with the sledge and I woke up to what he was about to do I quickly released the chisel and leapt from beside the barrel just as he made a blasting impact on the top of the barrel. "What are you doin' boy? You need to hold that thing for me!"

Typically, I am not the one to defy my grandfather, but on that day I was firmly convinced that he had completely parted company with his sense of reality. The only thing I could come up with was, "No way!"

"Aw, come on now. You know I ain't gonna' hit you and I need to cut the top of that barrel off," he pleaded with me.

"No way, you hold it and I'll swing." I really wasn't buying that there was a prayer that he would hit only that chisel. I had visions of my hand being turned to Jell-O, and I am kind of fond of my hand the way it is, thank you very much.

In the end, neither he nor I held the chisel, and neither one of us were swinging the sledge hammer. I honestly can't remember how the lid of that one eventually was sorted out, I am just thankful that the episode ended with all my digits intact. But, he did send me up on the roof of the house to put more sealant on the tin roof. I was much happier doing that with a 60 degree incline on a tin roof on the second story of the house than letting him take swings at my hand; it felt many times safer.

The Penhooker

There are a variety of reasons why we call people, things or
places the names that we do. Often in the ancient Hebrew tradition or
even in the Native American tradition, names mean something.
Abraham means father of a multitude, Jesus means will save, and here
Peniel means the face of God. These are all noble sounding and
meaning names, but we tend to lean towards less favorable names too
– like the names we give each other on the playground in elementary
school.

The more time I spent around my grandfather, the more it seemed
like he was stuck in kindergarten the way he acted. His terms, his
stubbornness, and his joviality were all examples of how he was stuck
in kindergarten, but on this day it was the names he used.

Visiting with Papaw in the summer was always a special treat. A
simple country man with simple country taste. Never was summer so
relaxing as when Papaw and I would spend it together. Rarely would
a conversation or activity become very deep. We always had plenty
to talk about, and plenty to do, but we never got in a hurry. It was just
country living at its best.

One of the activities that we always had to attend to was the
cattle. Normally, Papaw kept about fifty head of beef cattle and
regularly traded them and bought more. Never once did this take on
the high stakes type environment that seems so stereotypical of
farmers today. All trading was conducted under a large oak tree,
sitting in nylon webbing lawn chairs, and sipping on sweet tea. No
haggling or name calling ever occurred. Just polite conversation and
a handshake.

Papaw's reputation for being a fair man was well known
throughout Iredell County and it was not uncommon for people to

show up out of the blue to do business with him. Papaw was a farmer because he loved it, not to make money. Sure he made some money, but just what was fair, and just enough to keep his family taken care of; nothing more. As such it was not taken as out of the ordinary when Tom Simon showed up to purchase some cattle.

Papaw and I were sitting in the front yard, sipping on some ice tea, discussing the virtues of chewing tobacco. Papaw and I often had this discussion about, "worm medicine" as he called it. No amount of his nagging would get me to try it. It repulsed me just as much then as it does now. However, Papaw never let up. As a matter of fact we buried him with a pack of tobacco. While Papaw was explaining to me for about the fourth time that day how it could be used to soothe bee stings, Tom came riding up in a brand new pickup truck.

With Tom was an older gentleman, slightly stooped, carrying a wooden cane. Both were very congenial and greeted Papaw very warmly. Papaw immediately sent me for more lawn chairs and iced tea. When I returned with the chairs and iced tea we all sat around and discussed just about everything. We talked about the Braves. We talked about Papaw's days as a truck driver. We talked about how nice it was now that the road was paved. After a long time we finally got around to why Tom and his friend had showed up, which was to buy some cattle.

I was impressed with Tom. He was polished. He was smooth. There was no doubt in my mind that this man was a salesman. His companion, on the other hand, was down home country. A very simple man, of very few words. He quietly sipped on his iced tea, and didn't really contribute to the conversation; just an occasional chuckle or nod. However, Tom was smooth and tried to work his salesman tactics on Papaw, but he still paid just what anyone would for those calves.

I was always very happy with the way that Papaw never tried to exclude me from any adult conversation or activities. None of this conversation between him and Tom was any of my business, but I found it fascinating as I listened in. I was not even chastised for throwing in my two cents worth, even when I realize now that it really had no bearing on the conversations they were having. I was still stuck on the Braves when they had quietly moved on to the new paved road and my comments about Hank Aaron were just as welcome then as before.

Papaw and Tom talked for quite some time about just about everything. It was hard to even notice when the conversation slipped quickly to the calves he wanted to buy and the price that would be paid. That entire exchange lasted only about a minute in about an hour and a half conversation. Just as quickly as that portion of the conversation appeared, it disappeared. Only the most observant would have noticed the conversation that bore out about a $2,000 exchange. They quickly continued with their conversation about the Braves, the weather, or just about anything else. Shortly after that Tom and his companion got back into his new truck and rode away.

Papaw and I continued our daily regimen of working on various different projects around the farm, broken up by a grilled cheese sandwich and an episode of *All In The Family*. One thing that seemed to be never ending was the fence line. We set out across the pastures to the far reaches of the farm to repair some of the fence. Somehow it seemed that the further away the fence was from the house, the worse it was. We weren't really let down this time either. There was an old pine tree that had fallen on the fence leaving a wide opening that any cow could make it through. I would say that we began to work on it, but in reality I began to work on it. Papaw was great at convincing you that "we" were going to do something, but when it came down to it, it was only "I" that was swinging that axe. However, you know I really didn't mind. I was spending some time with a man that really meant the world to me. I was only too proud to swing that axe for him to clear that fence. While we worked that morning Papaw regaled me with his thoughts on the honorable profession of buying and selling cattle. He was so smooth at it though that I had no idea that he was not speaking very highly of the profession. He referred to Tom numerous times in the course of our conversation as a "penhooker". Unfortunately, I had no idea that it was not what you would consider flattering.

Later on that afternoon Tom returned because he and Papaw had agreed to go to the new meat packing house together. Now, for beef cattle farmers few things are more important than a new slaughter house. The new Cool Springs meat processing plant had just opened, and Tom was able to get us in for a grand tour.

Tom, Papaw, and I all piled into Tom's car and headed out to the new processing house. Papaw was truly in his element. He and Tom talked as if they had known each other since grade school, when Tom was really twenty years Papaw's junior. Papaw could make anyone feel at ease with his simple country charm and wit. Part of his wit was how he would try to seem like a big city man, when in reality he had rarely been outside Iredell County. Tom mentioned that a six-pack would make the trip to the processing plant much better, and of course Papaw couldn't agree more. Tom stopped just a couple miles down the road at a local Philips 66 and got a six-pack that he and Papaw shared. I will never forget the way that Papaw turned to me and said, "Now your Mamaw don't have to know about this boy." There was nothing like his devilish smile and loving way. Mamaw never did hear about the beer. Papaw and Tom finished their beers as we reached the processing plant. We walked in as if we owned the place and Tom proudly began to show us around.

Now, I had never really been to a meat processing plant before, so this was kind of eye opening. It seemed that no matter where we went there were carcasses hanging like obedient soldiers. Many chutes where cattle are lead on their final journeys. One particular room I remember was the room full of cow heads and organs. This, in no small way, was the most disgusting room I had ever seen, but also somewhat fascinating at the same time. It was such an odd pile of discarded cow parts strewn with their heads piled on top, their bodies hanging naked in the next room ready for stakes and Sunday roasts.

The next day Tom and his companion returned to collect the cattle that he had purchased the day before. As they were riding up into the driveway, I excitedly ran to tell Papaw about their arrival. I opened the screen door onto the back porch and shouted, "Papaw, that penhooker feller is here now."

Papaw moved quicker than I had ever seen to come near and quiet me down. He effectively grabbed me and told me, "Boy, don't be saying that now. It's not terribly flattering." Until that moment I had no idea that his comments the day before were not said in the best light of Tom.

Papaw and I had already locked the calves Tom was buying into the barn away from the other cattle. Some of these cows were not very happy about being locked up and as we began to try to load them onto Tom's truck they became even less happy. Each of us got a stick of some kind to help guide the cows. Tom's companion used his cane for his stick. I was dumbfounded when he warded off one of the cows from charging him with his cane. Tom's companion, even with his unsteady legs, deftly raised the cane and whacked the cow squarely between the eyes. That cow had no compunction about backing right down. After about an hour of something that could only be described as a Laurel and Hardy routine we finally got the cows loaded onto Tom's truck. With as little fanfare as when he first showed up, Tom and his companion were on their way, and I never saw the Penhooker again.

Wedding Weekend

On the third day there was a wedding in Cana of Galilee, and the mother of Jesus was there. Jesus and his disciples had also been invited to the wedding.

John 2:1-2

James and Tammy dated for years. Their love for each other as high school sweethearts is the stuff that romance novels are made of. As a matter of fact when they finally did finally get married many of us did not realize that they were not already married; you just never saw one without the other. However, when they did traverse the aisle together as husband and wife our family was there in force. Factors that came together that weekend highlight so much of the uniqueness of our family from our love, to our creativity, to our fun natured way of approaching life, and especially to our eccentricities; we are all just a bit out of round.

On most Sundays that little country church where James and Tammy exchanged their vows may hold 50 people if it is completely packed out. The Saturday of their wedding we packed over 200 friends and family into that little country church; testing the elasticity of the walls and pews. As we gathered we joked around and kidded one another about all sorts of things. One of our running jokes seems to always center around Jeff and Ryan.

Most family functions that Jeff and Ryan would attend, especially in their teen years, they would need to purchase a new suit because both of them were constantly growing. Usually one would wear the jacket with jeans and the other will wear the pants. Also, one will have their hair cut and the other will be growing it out to rival the length of Sampson. Since we never knew which would be which the rest of us take bets on who will be wearing the jacket and who will have their hair cut. As usual, however, they tend to throw a combination in that completely changes our dynamic. As unpredictable as Jeff and Ryan were about their appearance upon arrival, my father was equally predictable in his arrival; he will be late. The only variation for him is how late.

Wedding Weekend

On the day of the wedding a video camera was setup to capture all of the activity from the chancel area of the church so we could easily see their faces as they exchanged their vows. From that vantage point, though, it also captured activity in the congregation.

As the hour of the wedding approached my various cousins were all seated together in the same area of the church, along with some other relatives and friends. Each of their faces showed up clearly on the video that we all enjoyed after the wedding as we relived the day's events together later that evening. For some reason, I had been seated a few pews ways away from most of my cousins, but I began to notice in the video a significant amount of commotion among my cousins that seemed unusual for even them. From one person to the next I started to see them pass a handful of dollar bills down the pew in much too jovial of a manner. At first, I thought that they were taking up a collection for someone who had forgotten to bring a present so that they had a gift to give to James and Tammy. However, what really messed that theory up for me was when I saw on the video all the money go back down the pew to Kelley; and she was way too happy. I didn't grasp what was happening so I asked some of them who were watching the video with me what was going on.

What they told me left me in no small amount of shock, but also comfort with my family who were going to find fun at all costs. What I had missed was my father's entrance at the point the money was distributed. They had all taken bets on how late he would be, and Kelley placed the winning bet; who else but my family would be making bets in church. After the wedding and reception we all scattered in our own respective directions, invigorated by our time together again, and Kelley was buying.

The next day I had plans to meet my sister and my father for a meal together. As I pulled up to the restaurant, however, I was greeted by someone from the family telling me that Mamaw and Papaw had been in a car accident and that everyone had gone to the hospital to see about them. I immediately got back on the highway and joined them at the hospital out of deep concern for my grandparents.

When I arrived back in Iredell County the various details of their accident began to come into focus. Mamaw had been driving when the accident had occurred. She and Papaw were going to church, and, as per normal, they were arriving just before services were about to start. She had a practice of pulling up to the front door and dropping him off before parking the car. This day, however, as she made the hairpin turn into the parking lot her feet got twisted up in the pedals and rather than depress the brake she mistakenly depressed the gas pedal. The car rapidly accelerated from near zero to a speed that shook the entire church as she collided with the side of the building. Not only that, but the car was classified as a total loss in a distance of less than 50 yards.

Papaw's injuries were minor bumps and scrapes primarily from the airbag going off, but Mamaw's involved a badly sprained ankle. The thing that grieved her most, however, was the fact that she had also hit two teens about to enter the church as she careened toward the church; that wound she took with her to her grave.

Papaw's ability to care for himself had never been very good. He knew that he had an underwear drawer, but he wasn't quite sure where it was. He knew that food was prepared in the kitchen, and if any meal required more expertise than picking up a sandwich that was already made he was lost. As he got older all of that got even worse. Mamaw was very capable under normal circumstances, but not being able to move around the house without help was prohibitive for her doing anything on her own. Given these circumstances a decision was made that someone would stay with them each night for the next week or so. My turn came about the second or third night.

Staying with my grandparents was never a chore. I loved spending time with them on just about any occasion. I came up after I got off of work and prepared supper for them. We enjoyed a good meal and time together, even as a fairly blustery storm brewed up outside. As we completed our meal Mamaw went back to the den where she was able to put her foot up and talk with me while I cleaned up the kitchen. Papaw also sat down in the den.

As I worked on the dishes I noticed that Papaw had gotten up and wandered off to the back porch area where the restroom was. My thought was that he was going out there to do his business, but I began to hear him near the back door. The storm that had brewed up earlier had not declined any in the last hour, and had instead intensified. I was concerned that he was going to try to go outside in that storm without thinking about what he was doing.

I quickly made my way to the back porch to try to cut him off and noticed him standing near the back door, and it was not real evident what was going on. "Papaw, what are you doing?" I asked.

The answer I got back I was simply not prepared for. "I'm peeing in this can."

"You're doing what?!?" I asked incredulously

To which I got the quick and curt reply, "I'm peeing in this can then I'll pour it out the door."

I am still not sure how I maintained a straight face. "Oh," as if that happened every day. I stammered for a moment trying to figure out what on earth to do or say next. Meantime he finished up opened the door and tossed the contents of his can into the yard. I thought that perhaps I could at least add some sanitary content to this circus that I was witnessing, "Why don't we throw that can away now," as I reached for the can to toss it out.

"Nope," as he brushed past me and put the can on top of the freezer on the back porch; "I may need that later."

"But, Papaw, we do have indoor plumbing now," I desperately pleaded as he made his way back to the den.

He simply continued on his journey and dismissively waved me off. I guess I know where I stand now.

It is amazing how just a few events can lead to so much more than we ever bargained for. A wedding leading directly into gambling, car accidents, and an old man peeing in a can; who could have ever guessed? I suppose this is why you often hear, "truth is stranger than fiction."

Rook

But the steadfast love of the Lord is from everlasting to everlasting on those who
fear him, and his righteousness to children's children, to those who keep his
covenant and remember to do his commandments.

Psalm 103:17-18

There are certain activities that draw families together in a way
that simply spending time in the same dwelling never will.
Therapists, counselors, and just ordinary people tend to agree that
these family building activities are irreplaceable. At the top of the list
of these activities is going camping together or some other form of get
away where the distractions of the world are left behind. Another is
family games like board games and card games. It gives everyone the
opportunity to get involved and participate. In our family that game
was Rook.

Rook is a game that I have never actually seen anyone else play,
and I have never been able to find the particular rules (or lack thereof)
that we adhere to documented anywhere. For us, this is a case of
tribal wisdom; if you are part of the tribe the secrets of the game are
shared with you. When I have browsed through the various official
rules for Rook it appears that we have adopted the portions of those
rules that suited us, ignored the ones that don't, and made other stuff
up as we went along. However, it works for us.

My earliest memories certainly involve card tables being out for
various family functions. Usually, the card tables would be out
specifically for people to be able to eat, but they were not going to be
wasted the rest of the time they were up. Papaw always took a seat at
one of these tables and out came the Rook cards.

I both loved and dreaded being Papaw's partner, especially in his
later years. He was never a card shark or even one who was
moderately good at playing cards. He just played because he loved
doing it. When he held his cards they were not in the neatly splayed
fan that is typical of most card players, and nor were his cards sorted
in any kind of logical manner. Instead, his hand was nothing short of
a hot mess. Cards were barely holding on in his hand, while others
were hidden behind other cards. In the end, he had no idea what was

in his hand, but the rest of us sitting at the table could get a pretty good idea due to his lack of discipline in how he held his hand.

Typically, when playing any card game where the suits are important each player will prepare their hand at the beginning of that round to ensure they grouped the cards from a particular suit together. This practice also ensured that the player knew what cards they have in each suit. Papaw did none of that.

He often did muss about with his cards in his hand, but no one is very sure what organizational pattern he was following. Yet, despite his disorganization he was actually able to do relatively well, but it required a lot of patience and forgiveness by everyone at the table.

When playing Rook it is important to follow the suit led for each trick with the same suit; you cannot play off-suit unless you do not have any cards of the suit that was led. This is where it is critical that you are organized in your thoughts, and where Papaw experienced the greatest challenges. If, for instance, black was named as trumps but green was led for that trick you must play green if you have it; you cannot play any other color, including trumps, unless you do not have green. Inevitably, however, Papaw would have one of those green cards tucked in behind another card because of the way he held his hand and would not know it, so he would throw down a trump card to take the trick. As his partner, this excited me; we took a trick. Of course, he would lead off the next trick with the green card he had just missed having in his hand much to everyone's consternation.

Papaw and either shuffling or dealing was always exciting to witness. The older he got the more arthritis crept into his reality and the harder it was for him to be able to successfully manipulate the cards, but even much younger there was no doubt that he was not a card shark. More or less, the cards would get shuffled, and more or less, they would also get dealt. Cards would be in random directions with very random results. Some players may have different numbers of cards and the same with the kitty. We would often resolve this by not even looking at the cards he was dealing until he was done so that we could count the cards and sort out any shortfalls in advance.

Later on, Papaw would graciously allow one of us to shuffle the cards for him, which actually turned out relatively well. We would shuffle and hand the cards back to him, and as long as we did not distract him the cards more or less ended up where they were supposed to.

Whenever Mamaw was watching us we definitely took things to another level. A cruel reality for many men and women of a certain age is the challenges of bladder control. A cruel reality of grandchildren is the challenge as they see it of causing their grandparent to lose bladder control by the laughter that would be generated in their vicinity. Mamaw was one of those whose bladder control was a challenge that we heartily took that challenge on.

When Mamaw watched, the hijinks at and around the table increased exponentially; of course, it was already pretty high. We played with joy and enthusiasm and made sure that we poked enough fun at one another that Mamaw would begin to laugh, and she loved to laugh. The goofier and weirder we were the more she laughed, and the more she laughed the more often she was dashing for the rest room. She would come back a couple of minutes later with, "Now y'all stop that," laughing again even as she spoke.

No matter which Connolly household you visit, laughter is a significant component of our family life. Normally, this is well-received and appreciated; unless, of course, you just had abdominal surgery.

As my sister-in-law discovered, our home was a comfortable place to recover from surgery as long as no laughter ensued. That proved to be a challenge far too great, and she didn't help her cause much either because she provided plenty of laughable material herself.

After her surgery when she was released from the hospital she came to live with us for a couple of weeks. We always enjoy having her in our home, and she gets swept up into the normal laughter and banter around our home. Usually, it was just a chuckle here or there but on one particular occasion it was laughter that was epic in proportion, and, of course that coincided with abdominal surgery.

Out of a sense of self-preservation, Lizzy stayed down stairs in our home. Doing this she had her own bedroom, bathroom, and sitting area. She also had free access to the wood burning stove, and since it was over the Christmas break this was a highly coveted position. Although she could traverse the stairs she rarely did because it was simply too painful at first.

During one of our family meals my wife, daughter and I were sitting at the table and my wife thought she heard her sister and wanted to go check on her to ensure she was OK. Emma began to descend the stairs, but did not quite make it all the way down before I saw her running back up the stairs with her hand over her mouth. I wasn't sure of what was going on, and didn't know if something had gone horribly wrong. I quickly realized that the tears streaming down her face were tears of laughter, the hand over her mouth was to suppress the snorts of laughter, and she ran to the back of the house to compose herself out of earshot of her sister. Meanwhile, Lizzy was trying to regain her composure as well so that she could breathe again because of her own laughter.

It took some time for either of them to gather themselves up enough to convey what had happened, but it was nothing short of epic. When Emma descended the stairs she glimpsed upon a vision of her sister warming herself near the wood stove. Because of the many sutures she tended to be sparse with what she wore under her robe, but neatly kept her robe tucked around her to cover herself. However, she discovered that if she backed up to the stove she could lift the back of her robe and warm her bum in an ever so pleasant manner. Upon seeing this, and after having hung out around me for way too long, Emma's thoughts immediately went to, "I hope she doesn't fart."

Lizzy is cut from the same fabric of DNA as Emma. Often, their thoughts are in synch with one another in a scary way; this was one of those occasions. No words were spoken. Only a glance was exchanged. Both were in hysterics.

So, the bottom line from all this is enjoy your family time, laughter is awesome and healing, and it is what is needed to share around the game table to build those bonds. However, if you have bladder control issues or you are recovering from abdominal surgery, don't stay with a Connolly. Find the most boring person you can think of and stay there, but when you are ready for a good laugh, break out the Rook cards and take a seat with the Connolly's; its healing in a whole new way.

The rules of Rook – the Connolly version:

- Rook is a card game with 4 players, divided into two teams. The partners for each team should sit opposite to each other so that as you go around the table you would have team 1 player 1, team 2 player 1, team 1 player 2, and team 2 player 2. How you choose your teams is your own stinkin' problem.
- The deck of Rook cards is prepared by removing the 2's, 3's, & 4's from the deck. Don't ask; I don't know why. Certain things we just do them that way.
- A dealer is chosen for the first hand, and then subsequently rotates around the table to the dealer's left for the next dealer. How you choose the first one again is your own stinkin' problem. There are no rules for this part; actually there may be but we simply make it up as we go along.
- The dealer will deal 10 cards to each player and 5 to the kitty in the center of the table. Although strict adherence to good order and discipline to Rook aficionados would dictate an orderly laying out of cards, in a clockwise order, and every second round adding a card to the kitty that ain't happening here. Eventually, every player will have their 10 cards, and eventually 5 will end up in the kitty – don't get bound up in proper card etiquette it will simply give you ulcers.
- The last card laid down should be the final card to the kitty. But, again, don't get wrapped up in it happening in just that way. Also, in these rule it is allowed, and often expected, that the final card on the kitty will be face up. It is done for intrigue. It is done since most everyone is pitiful at handling cards so by the time you get to the last card all the other players have probably seen it anyway. It is done out of "Tradition! Tradition!" (think "Fiddler on the Roof")
- Once all the cards are dealt the player to the dealer's left will make the opening bid, anywhere from "pass" to "Shoot the Moon". The maximum points available in a hand is 180. Of course, you can lose every trick and end

up with zero. Scoring will be discussed below, however, when you bid you do so with enthusiasm, especially if you shoot the moon, and most especially if you have an absolutely pitiful hand. To shoot the moon means you will take every point available, all 180 points. You may find some sticklers for the rules who insist that you must take every trick, but they are just boring and don't know how we do things. Of course, when you do take the bid you are effectively writing a check that your partner has to cash. All bids should be in increments of multiples of 5 or 10.

- Talking across the table is highly discouraged, but tends to happen anyway – so again, get over yourself. No great state secrets are shared, but you certainly figure out how to communicate with your partner as you talk about farm machinery and the Braves. If you need to ask which Braves or who the Braves are you probably don't want to play at our table; just sayin'.

- The person who takes the bid has the option of showing the kitty to the table; this really is our version of smack talk. Don't even bother trying to find that in a rule book – it ain't there. They take the five cards into their hand and discard any five cards they wish into the hold cards; these are very important later on. The strategy here is to make your hand as strong as possible and remove any weaknesses. Since you get to name the trump suit you probably want to have as many trump cards in your hand as possible. The remaining cards should all also be winners as much as possible.

- Play begins with the person who took the bid, and they also name the trump suit (green, black, red, or yellow). There are, of course, truly weird people who may choose to name trumps as "no trump", which means the only trump card is the Rook card itself. The trump suit trumps other cards played, and unless a higher value trump card is played by a subsequent player then the player who played the trump card wins that trick. The person who won the bid can play any card in their hand they choose –

it's good to be the king. Subsequent players must play the same suit that led unless they do not have any of that suit, in which case they are free to play whatever they choose. What they choose may be in an effort to add or deny points as a strategy, and that will be discussed more below.

- In each suit there are cards 1, and 5-14 (remember you took out 2-4). The highest card in rank is 1, then 14 down. The one exception to this is the Rook card itself; it is the highest card in the named trump suit.
- The points are as follows:
  - Rook = 20 points
  - 1's = 15 points
  - 14's and 10's = 10 points
  - 5's = 5 points
- One of the two players on each team should collect the tricks won since you are functioning as a team after all. Obviously, your objective is to win every trick, as a team. Part of winning is getting points and you need to take as many points as possible. If your partner is winning a trick and you can play cards with points into his / her trick – do it. At the end of each round of play you add up the points in the tricks you have won. The team who won the last trick gets whatever is in the hold cards that the person who won the bid puts aside.
- If you do not make your bid then you get negative whatever points were bid. Otherwise, you get the points that your team acquired during play.
- The team who gets to 500 first wins. That is unless you make up the rules as you go along like we do and that can be any number you choose.

OK, so that's our rules. We don't play to beat each other down; we play to enjoy each other's company. Oh, and yeah, we do reserve the right to change the rules to suit us – it's just the way we roll because no matter what we are going to have fun and level the playing field so that the youngest to the oldest is able to have fun.

Biltmore

The silver is mine, and the gold is mine, says the Lord of hosts. The latter splendor
of this house shall be greater than the former, says the Lord of hosts; and in this
place I will give prosperity, says the Lord of hosts.

Haggai 2:8-9

Even though Papaw felt that he had all of the culture he needed right there in Iredell County, we still felt compelled to take him to Biltmore House in Asheville, NC. Biltmore House will never be the same again, and I know that we won't.

Biltmore is a gorgeous estate, built by George Vanderbilt near Asheville, NC. Construction on this incredible home began in 1889, but was not complete until 1895; six years to build one home. Its vast expanse overlooks a significant portion of the Smokey Mountains and provides a picturesque view of the land that the Lord gave us to watch over. The Vanderbilt's left no luxury out of this house, and its opulence is a thing of legend. Many people from around the world visit it each year, in its many seasons, to enjoy the grandeur of it and compare it to their own humble dwellings. Biltmore puts on a particularly spectacular display around Christmas with decorations, and choirs, and mulled ciders. The Christmas season is when we chose to take Papaw to Biltmore.

As we entered the estate, it was magical. The weather was gorgeous, the house was impeccably decorated, and we were enjoying the gift of family to its fullest. The long lawn leading up to the front door was cut and clean as only a professional organization could keep it. Biltmore even provided a long series of tents that were heated for us to be in while we waited in line to get our tickets. It seemed that nothing was too good for Biltmore's guests. The wait was long, but it wasn't unpleasant. We discussed the weather, the beauty of the estate, what Tommy was doing with the cows now, and what we were going to do for lunch.

Mamaw still got around fairly well, but Papaw had problems with his knees and his mobility was somewhat diminished. As we entered the house, we convinced Papaw to ride in a wheelchair so that it would not be so difficult on his knees. This actually lasted most of the day with us pushing him from room to room; much longer than any of us really expected. Papaw would give us directions of where he wanted to go with his usual grunts, pointing, and waving his hand, and we would oblige so that he could see what he wanted.

We gently strolled from room to room, looking at the beautiful arrangements and accoutrements in each room. Each room had its own unique design and theme, and, as a result, its own unique decoration for Christmas. Papaw did not quite appreciate all of the work that they put into it as much as he just enjoyed being with his family. Papaw did try, but he tired very quickly.

As he tired his patience also waned, and his desire to stay in the wheelchair diminished. Finally, by the time we got to the third floor he had had as much of that wheelchair as he could stand, and out he came. He got along fairly well, to be as tired as he was. Luckily, the pace of the procession of people through the rooms on that floor was quite slow. We would move 5 or 10 feet then wait for a minute or so then move another 5 or 10 feet.

In the trips that I had made to Biltmore prior to this visit I had never had the opportunity to visit this third floor. It had only recently been opened to the public, and even then, only small portions of it had. The wooden paneling and the wooden floor were especially nice. They gave the place a nice majestic feel, and the scent of the wood paneling just added to the ambiance. The sensation of walking through the halls of history in a grand legal library was breathtaking. Each footstep echoed through the halls, and the subtle creek of the floor under foot was audible even with this many people there. However, Papaw did not fully appreciate the intricate work that had been put into building this grand section of the house. Instead he tired even more rapidly and longed to get outside and sit down for a while. Unfortunately, at that moment we were more or less trapped until the line cleared up some.

We moved along as rapidly as we could for Papaw's sake, but we could only move so fast. At one particular point we stopped for a moment in a mahogany colored alcove. The wood and the carving in it were magnificent. The musty smell of the wood was breathtaking, and the echo in this portion was even more than before. Even the most subtle whisper would carry great distances.

Papaw leaned against one of the great walls of the alcove and was visibly tired. He mentioned something about his knees aching and wiped his brow. Then, he hiked a leg and provided for the enjoyment of all one almighty fart. I would like to say that he passed gas, but that doesn't come close to doing it justice. The bass tone rumble that came from his south end could only be described as a fart; there's really no delicate way to put it. And boy did it echo. There was no doubt in anyone's mind on the third floor of Biltmore that day what he had just done, and even less doubt as to where it had come from.

Then Mamaw began to laugh. Really, it was all she could do. Papaw showed no remorse; instead he only showed relief. Her laughter was refreshing to see, unlike the air we were in at the time. Mamaw laughed so hard and so long that she nearly lost control of her bladder. It was all we could do to get them both to a bathroom before we had a very unpleasant trip back home that evening. However, we did arrive at the facilities in time and all was well. Biltmore House will never be the same in anyone's mind from the third floor that day, and perhaps that day is why the third floor is rarely open to visitors even now.

Cheer for your team

David danced before the LORD with all his might; David was girded with a linen ephod.

2 Samuel 6:14

Before this story begins, I must make a confession. I intentionally did not use the actual name of some individuals in this story. This was done out of deep and abiding love and sympathy for those involved because they have clearly suffered enough.

David was often referred to as a man after God's own heart. Yet, he often was a warrior, a lover, an adulterer, a murderer, and a liar. Still, David's dance before the Lord, I believe, was one of those events that God took great pleasure in. David was not ashamed of his love for the Lord at all, and saw the return of the Ark of the Covenant as a tremendous blessing on God's people by God. In thanks and praise for all that God had done David danced, and in great joy he essentially danced in his underwear. David was not dancing to be titillating or vulgar; instead he danced the dance of a man that was truly thankful to God. David's heart was in keeping with God's.

Papaw was never the king of Israel, or even of Iredell County. He was the prince, to be sure, of his own land. The Ark of the Covenant never passed through his living room, but an occasional Braves game did. David danced for joy and so did Papaw, and for both men it certainly raised eyebrows. There can be little doubt, however, of the genuineness of either man's joy or elation.

There are not many games like baseball that inspires the loyalty that it has. Baseball goes back for generations with entire families showing a common loyalty to a given team. Even the Civil War did not show that kind of loyalty within a family. Families take their loyalties to a particular team very seriously, and families have had significant squabbles over who would inherit the season tickets at certain parks. Others have had significant rifts develop all because some family members expressed a loyalty to another team by something as mundane as accepting a job in that other team's hometown.

Papaw was a Braves man, and beyond that a National League man. Visiting him in the summers, he and I would discuss all manner of things, but always seemed to come back to baseball. His commentary on the fans was just as colorful as his commentary on the game. I once heard him refer to a fan chewing a wad of gum as looking like, "a horse chewing a mouth full of briars." I suppose he must have actually witnessed that in the past, but I certainly never have.

One summer he and I were discussing the fact that he had been to a number of the ball parks around the country, how he got to go, and what he remembered about it. Usually, these visits coincided with his days as a truck driver. He would ensure that his arrival at the truck terminal corresponded with a particular game so that as his truck was loaded or unloaded he would venture across the street or around the corner to watch the game. That particular summer the New York Yankees were doing quite well, and I asked Papaw if he had ever been to see them play.

His initial response was in the look he had on his face of absolute righteous indignation that I could ever utter something so foul in his presence. How could I possibly utter something so vulgar about his behavior? He was not so upset that I had proposed that he had gone to see the Yankees play, but that I had suggested he might have been to an American League park or worse yet be an American League fan. There was no ambiguity in his loyalties at all as he responded, "I am a National League man."

Later in his years, Papaw's enthusiasm for doing a number of tasks waned. Pretty much any task that required movement from him was a challenge to impose on him. Paramount in this list was getting a bath. Mamaw would beg and plead to get him moving and to make his way to the shower. Usually, Mamaw resorted to bribery and / or extortion (both are excellent qualities for a Christian grandmother to possess and use) in order to convince the man, stubborn as he was, to wash the filth from his body.

One year, late in the baseball season, the Braves were looking great. Their possibilities for a pennant and the World Series were exceptionally good, and Papaw was beside himself. The pennant race was close and a season decider was on, but Papaw still needed to bathe. Normally Papaw showered, but this evening, after much debate, coercion, and bribery, Mamaw was able to convince Papaw that he could listen to the game from the other room as he bathed if Mamaw turned the TV volume up. Both parties reluctantly agreed, and set about their tasks.

The whole scene was quite comical. Papaw's hearing was such that the volume had to be turned up to the point that the neighbors about a half a mile away could easily determine the fate of the game as well. All of the interconnecting doors in the house were opened so as not to impede the status of the game from making it to Papaw.

As the game progressed it became a real nail-biter. The score was tied in the late innings of the game, with the Braves up to bat. The first batter up was walked, so now the winning run in on first. Papaw's interest just got peaked, and now he is sitting up a little taller in the tub. The batter and the pitcher bantered back and forth with a volley of foul balls, strikes, and balls. Each time the batter connected for another foul Papaw eased closer to the edge of the tub as the color announcer called the game. The atmosphere was absolutely electric.

Finally, the batter connected for a long fly ball, and Papaw made his way out of the tub ensuring that he didn't miss even a moment of the precious game. Inch by inch, as the color commentator called the play, Papaw made his way closer to the game. When the ball cleared the outfield fence Papaw was standing in the hallway, dripping wet, jumping up and down for joy. Papaw was so happy and so enthralled in the game that he had never even heard the knock on the door.

Miss Hazel was a lovely lady in her late sixties. She and Mamaw were in the same circle at the Methodist church together, and often Miss Hazel would lead the Bible studies for their circle or help coordinate some of the activities that they did. Today she was preparing for a study based on John 4, the story of the woman at the well, as well as coordinating some of the refreshments for their next meeting tomorrow.

When she arrived at the old farmhouse, she didn't think it all that odd that the TV was loud, although it did seem to be a bit louder than usual; after all, the elderly couple that lived there were a bit hard of hearing. As was customary, when she arrived she went to the back door, since only door-to-door salesmen ever used the front door.

Now Miss Hazel had been through many things in her life. She had seen a lot, and experienced much of what life has to offer. But, nothing could have fully prepared her for the scene she was walking into. At the old farmhouse, knocking on the door was simply a formality before walking in to say hello. Formality, of any form, had never been a part of my grandparents' household. Hazel, following tradition, knocked on the door, but she was certain that due to the volume of the TV that no one had heard her knock so she stepped up and into the house. Just as she got through the door and had it closed behind her, a wet, naked, eighty-year-old man came tearing out of the bathroom, jumping up and down, and hollering like a wild man. This was almost more than her heart could take.

Hazel had just learned more about my grandfather than she had ever wanted to know. The entire crowd, Mamaw, Papaw, and Hazel were all in stitches and bright red. Hazel was confident that there are certain things in life that are better left to the imagination, and all she could seem to do was remember the words to a Ray Stevens song, "Oh, yes, they call him the Streak...He likes to show off his physique." No matter how hard she tried, she could not find a way that this would help her to complete her Bible study preparation. Also, no matter how hard she tried she could not figure how she would ever look at Papaw with a straight face again at church.

Marion's Teeth

Then our mouth was filled with laughter, and our tongue with shouts of joy then it was said among the nations, "The LORD has done great things for them."

Psalm 126:2

Auntie Marion rocked; there just isn't a better way to put it. She was one of the most unique people that I ever met. She had an independent streak that would give the Great Wall of China a run for its money. Her genuine love for her family and her simple country ways made her a true pleasure to be around.

Marion was one of my wife's aunts from North Yorkshire in England. The people of North Yorkshire, where my wife's family comes from, and the people of Iredell County in North Carolina, where my family comes from, both supposedly speak English. The likelihood of either of these groups understanding each other would be quite slim, however. Both groups do speak English, but combining the dialect and the extremely strong accents of each would make the conversation between the two something that should be a spectator event; sell tickets. It would probably be the only event you would go to that would require translators with both people speaking the same language.

Marion was a frugal and self-sufficient woman that would rarely, if ever, ask another human being for assistance. Much of that attitude, as with many people of her generation, comes from her experiences during World War II.

WWII was devastating to the British people. The German blitzkriegs and the rationing of basic daily staples changed that generation in ways that still persist seventy years later. Only the lights that were absolutely imperative to be on were, and there was certainly talk about what absolutely imperative actually meant. Sugar, tea, coffee, etc. were all rationed, and families were only allotted a certain amount. Things they had once taken for granted were now at a premium to get. As a result, Marion and the rest of her generation began to learn to do without and tighten their belts a few notches in support of the war efforts.

The typical way of taking tea in England is with a little milk and a little sugar. As with coffee, some people want both, some want neither, and some want only one or the other; it is a personal taste. The prevailing presumption, however, is that everyone takes both milk and sugar. This is not much different from my own Iredell County where the assumption is that you drink your iced tea sweet, and unsweetened tea is almost seen as uncivilized.

On a trip to visit Marion, my wife was enjoying a pot of tea with her at a local garden. A number of people were there at the same time, and table space became a premium. My wife and Marion shared a larger table with some other ladies at the garden that afternoon, but had no real interaction with them. For more than half an hour Marion and my wife chatted and enjoyed the wonderfully crisp afternoon in refreshing North Yorkshire air.

After a while, my wife asked Marion if she would like some more tea. Marion did, and as typical English custom, my wife politely offered to add milk and sugar to her tea for Marion. Marion said, "Milk please dear, but no sugar." My wife, Emma, complied with no questions.

The other ladies they were sharing the table with, however, were not about to be silent. For almost an hour now, Marion and the other ladies had barely acknowledged each other's presence. Emma thought they were strangers who were cordially sharing their table, until one of them spoke up. "So, you don't take sugar in your tea do ya, Marion?"

In an air that explained it all, Marion replied, "No, not since war." At that point, the other ladies understood perfectly, and my wife was dumbfounded. She was dumbfounded over the fact that Marion and these ladies had known each other since they were children, but barely acknowledged each other. She was also dumbfounded over the fact that, "No, not since war," seemed to explain everything.

Because of sugar rationing in WWII, many people began to learn to take their tea without sugar. The little sugar there was had been reserved for other more important things like supporting the British soldiers and sailors, or canning of fruit for later use. With those others being the primary use, tea began to take a back seat on the list of things that sugar went into. Once Marion adapted to that philosophy and learned to do without, continuing that way was no problem. Since the other lady was of the same generation, she of course needed no further explanation. She also need no explanation of which war, for to nearly all of North Yorkshire of a certain generation there really is only one war to which they may refer – World War II.

Marion's sense of independence was just as staunch as her sense of frugality. Although her life may be in danger, Marion would insist on doing and helping no matter what. It is one of those qualities that would both endear you to Marion and frustrate you about her.

In Marion's later years she often needed the assistance of a cane to keep herself steady. Even at that, she still enjoyed puttering around in her garden with various flowers and shrubs that would make most people in America green with envy. Her home was only about 100 years old, so it is relatively new by British standards. Her garage was the old coal shed, and on her property is what remains of an old Quaker church that hasn't been in use for many years. Each of these aspects added a certain charm and character that is only present in these wonderful country homes in North Yorkshire. With the charm, however, come certain dangers of older equipment and the like being around.

Beside the old coal shed was an old radiator leaning up against the building. Marion's insistence on doing things for herself, found her cleaning up around the old coal shed and trying to reposition this old radiator. In the process, the rusty piece of equipment lost balance and toppled onto Auntie Marion, pinning her to the ground. The falling radiator also caused significant damage to Marion's leg, and her future on this earth was looking bleak.

The unshakeable Marion, however, being the stubborn Yorkshire lass that she was, was not about to let a little thing like a 200 pound radiator and a leg bleeding profusely slow her down. Using her cane, she resourcefully pried the radiator up and off her as she slid from beneath it. For a fifty-year-old person this would have been an impressive feat, but for a ninety-year-old woman this was beyond normal human belief. It did take her a significant amount of time as well pinned under that old radiator as she was, but she was stalwart in her approach. Meantime, she continued to lose a significant amount of blood from her wounded leg, and that old rusty equipment mixed with a ninety-year-old leg was simply an infection looking for a place to happen. Eventually, Marion prevailed and the radiator was vanquished, but the radiator had won a significant battle in the war.

Marion's leg was severely injured and required her to be hospitalized to repair the damage and allow her the space to heal. The healing process was no easy task, even for this stubborn North Yorkshire woman. Her leg became infected and required more aggressive treatment and more from her body to help it to heal. Unfortunately, some of this had the added side effect of nausea. Marion was still the self-sufficient woman and found a bucket just in the nick of time to prevent making a larger mess.

Hospital nursing staffs in England are nothing if not efficient. After Marion's bought with nausea she rested quietly while the nurse took her partially filled bucket and emptied it quietly and efficiently. The nurse's plan was to clean the bucket and bring it back just in case Marion had another round of nausea, all without disturbing Marion's peaceful slumber.

The nurse emptied the bucket into what the British refer to as a sluice, or a garbage disposal. When the nurse engaged the motor for the sluice, the noise it made left a sick feeling in the pit of that nurse's stomach. She quickly switched it off, but the damage was already done. She searched feverishly to determine the source of the horrible grinding noise, and pulled from the sluice what looked like little white bits of bone. Soon the nurse came to realize that she had just ground Marion's teeth into oblivion. In a panic of not knowing what else to do, the nurse feverishly retrieved all of the broken bits of Marion's dentures from the sluice, and placed them in a cup. She cleaned them, and then returned Marion's teeth to her. The largest pieces in the cup were the individual porcelain teeth themselves.

Marion was just beginning to realize that she could not find her teeth when the nurse returned. Together they then realized that her teeth had been expelled from her mouth into the bucket during her latest round of nausea and that now her teeth were proudly sitting before her in a coffee cup. Marion didn't know whether to laugh or cry, so she just laughed and said, "Thank you dear." Of course, how else would you respond if someone were to hand you a cup full of your own teeth.

Marion continued to chuckle about that for the balance of her days. The nurse's kindness and tenderness were not lost on Marion. Actually, Marion felt sorry for the young lady, and knew how ashamed of what she had done she was. However, Marion never missed a beat and was able to forgive and love the young nurse beyond the simple mistake. Besides, it gave Marion and the rest of the family a great story that is worth much more than the price of a set of dentures.

Papaw's Teeth

For everything there is a season, and a time for every matter under heaven: a time to be born, and a time to die; a time to plant, and a time to pluck up what is planted; a time to kill, and a time to heal; a time to break down, and a time to build up; a time to weep, and a time to laugh; a time to mourn, and a time to dance; a time to throw away stones, and a time to gather stones together; a time to embrace, and a time to refrain from embracing; a time to seek, and a time to lose; a time to keep, and a time to throw away; a time to tear, and a time to sew; a time to keep silence, and a time to speak; a time to love, and a time to hate; a time for war, and a time for peace.

Ecclesiastes 3:1-8

There is a season for everything under heaven as we read in Ecclesiastes. As is true in most lives we often see more of one side of this equation than the other. We would like to think that there is a balance and there will be just as much laughing as there is weeping, but it doesn't always work out that way. Papaw experienced this too, specifically for him, losing. He spent a significant portion of his life losing things, and we spent much of ours seeking them.

I believe that Papaw even began to find a level of humor in this situation himself. When I was in my 20's I was staying at the farmhouse for the night with my grandparents. As was our normal routine we ate dinner, watched a little TV, and then close to bedtime we all seemed to gravitate toward the kitchen for no particular reason. Several of us were talking about the day's events and only moderately embellishing our greatness in the process. Meanwhile, I noticed Papaw doing something that looked a little odd out of the corner of my eye. I didn't quite catch what he was doing, but it looked like he put something upon on the window sash and it didn't make any sense to me. "Papaw, what are you doing?" I inquired.

"I'm a takin' my watch off and puttin' it up here," he replied as if he did that every day.

Still not quite getting it, I asked, "Why you doin' that?"

"It gives me somethin' to do in the mornin'"

"Oh, ok," as if I actually understood what he was talking about, "what's that?"

"Find my watch," as he placed it at the back end of the window sash.

Papaw, like many adults of his generation, wore false teeth. However, he never really grasped the concept of how to keep up with where his teeth were. The places they ended up over the years became a thing of legend. There are two particular cases, however, that seem to top them all.

Although Papaw had false teeth, he rarely put them in his mouth. More often than not, he would put them somewhere for safekeeping, and then end up forgetting where he left them. One of his favorite places for putting his teeth so that he would remember where they were was his shirt pocket, but even that was tough to remember, and often problematic.

Papaw and Mamaw often took journeys to visit family and friends all across the region. On one trip they were going to visit my uncle, Bill, and his family on the other side of the state. Every trip for Papaw and Mamaw, even to the grocery store, required meticulous planning and preparation. Papaw would check the gas; luckily the days of having to do that with a stick had passed. He would check the tire pressure. He would check the oil level; the days of a stick are still here for this one. He would check the battery water level, and make sure that the windshield washer fluid was full. No check was left undone, and that was just to go to the grocery store. You can just imagine how much effort he went to in order to drive three hours to my uncle's home. With all that checked, and an old frozen concentrate orange juice can for a spittoon in hand, he was ready for a trip of any length.

Mamaw and Papaw climbed into the car and headed out down the highway. Usually, they would stop about half way for a bathroom break, and another meticulous check of the car's systems. Papaw would wonder around, strike up a conversation with the station attendant, pick up a few sticks (another story for another time), check the oil and get back on the road. Nothing was different on this trip. About halfway to my uncle's, they stopped for their usual break and Papaw made his usual checks then they were back on the road. He would drive, Mamaw would scold him about how fast he was going, and he would ignore her; everything situation normal.

A couple of hours later they arrived at my uncle's. No greeting was complete without plenty hugs and kisses. My uncle and my cousins helped unload their suitcases, while Papaw settled in on the back porch with a nice tall glass of iced tea; and yes, of course the tea here is sweetened – how else would we drink it. Papaw would settle in and survey the garden. He closely scrutinized the garden to ensure that the potatoes and the onions were placed in proper proximity to one another. Otherwise, the onion would get in the potato's eyes and make it cry. Papaw would enjoy telling my uncle about how well his tomatoes were starting to come in, and how beautiful the new calf was back home. Papaw's garden and his cattle were a constant source of pride for him.

Sometime later, my aunt announced that dinner was ready. Although Papaw always enjoyed eating, never once did he partake in the preparation of the meal, and definitely not the cleaning up afterwards. This to him, of course, was woman's work, and he had no part of that. Upon the announcement of the dinner bell, Papaw and my uncle started making their way in to the table. Papaw would always pull his wad of Red Man chewing tobacco out of his mouth and throw it into the yard. Then he would hack and spit and sputter to get the last remnants of tobacco from his mouth – no doubt this was a tremendous source of embarrassment and amusement for my aunt and my cousins. Papaw would then reach into his pocket, retrieve his teeth, and put them in. Everything went well until this last step when his teeth weren't in his pocket where they were expected to be.

An all-out search was launched to find the teeth. Papaw was such a creature of habit that it was only a matter of time before the elusive teeth would either be found, or determined to be part of the garden where he would have inevitably plowed them under as had happened to so many other sets of teeth, wallets, and other items of importance. Everyone was fairly confident that the teeth had fallen from his pocket, so they started retracing his steps. They checked the bathroom, and yes in the toilet too – no luck. They checked around the garden – no luck. They checked between the cushions on the sofa – no luck. They checked his jacket pocket – no luck. They checked the trunk of the car – no luck. They checked the driver's compartment – no luck. They were about to give up when my grandmother remembered that Papaw had previously checked the oil.

They thought that it was crazy to consider that possibility, but they tried anyway, and wouldn't you know it there were a set of uppers there – probably not something that most mechanics would expect to find under the hood of a Buick, but they don't know Papaw. The last time that he had checked the oil the teeth had fallen from his pocket and landed on the wheel well of the car, and had somehow stayed put for another two hours of driving. The people that talk about a cat riding on the wheel well for two hours think they have something.

Just as if nothing had ever happened, Papaw took the teeth, said thank you, ran a small amount of water over them and popped them in. Nothing ever really fazed him when it came to his teeth; he just rolled with the punches. Then he sat down and enjoyed another terrific meal that my aunt, Eunice, had prepared.

Papaw's teeth disappearing, and not noticed until it was time to eat, was not confined to travel. He could just as easily stay within the confines of his home and completely lose track of them. It could either be just him and my grandmother there, or the entire clan could be gathered for Thanksgiving lunch and they would disappear just as quickly. No event was too mundane or too sacred for the elusive teeth to go missing yet once more.

Thanksgiving is always a time when our family gathers to give thanks to God for all his bountiful blessings. The common love our family shares is a bond that few actually understand, even us. Some of us may not have seen each other for a year or more, but it is as if we never were separated when we come back together to break bread, say prayers, and enjoy the fellowship of our family. All of the cousins are as close as brother and sister, and each cousin has multiple parents in the respective aunts and uncles. Family gatherings, like this, are never complete without adding in some of our close friends as well. Friends that spend Thanksgiving with us are never disappointed with the camaraderie or the food. The stories that we share around the table with those gathered have become part of our family lore, and at least a good portion of them are even true. These friends that gather with us are usually taken aback by the closeness of such an extended family that they don't know what to do, but we do – we love them. They arrive as strangers and are always shown more love than they have ever experienced. Then they clamor to return with us again and again; only as close as family after that in love.

Even though there are forty or more people gathered for lunch, we all try to gather in the kitchen for our prayer. We spend what seems to be an interminable amount of time trying to squeeze forty people into a space designed for five. We join hands, and offer up a prayer of Thanksgiving for such a wonderful family and for all that God has given us. Then we depart from the divine and demonstrate gluttony and savagery to new heights, all except Papaw.

Papaw would calmly go find his chair and sit down. My grandmother, being the saint that she was, would prepare a plate for him and bring it to him. She would make sure that he had his knife and fork, his napkin, and his glass of iced tea. Then she would find her way back to the kitchen to worry about everyone else but herself. Eventually, she would find her own way to the table to enjoy her lunch, which would rarely feed even a small bird. However, this time she noticed that Papaw was not eating when she gave him his lunch. He simply sat there with a tremendously forlorn face and didn't eat. Mamaw quietly held his arm and said, "Philip, what's wrong?"

In words that I will never forget, Papaw responded, "I can't find my teeth."

As sad as it was, it was still humorous. Actually, the collective eruption of laughter convinced our guests that day that we were a bunch of heartless sadists to laugh at the misfortune of that "poor old man;" oh, if they only knew. However, at the time, it wasn't very funny to Papaw. He had a beautiful plate of food in front of him, and no way to do anything about it; he was defenseless. My grandmother, God bless her, was a resourceful woman. She announced, "I got a hundred dollars for the first grandbaby that finds Papaw's teeth." She knew from previous experience, way too many times, that they cost $200 to replace.

There really is nothing quite like the allure of a "C" note to get my cousins moving. All of us started searching. We looked everywhere. I had cousins searching all of the seat cushions, the beds, the trashcan, the toilet, and even the burn barrel. We knew our Papaw, the crazy things he would do, the crazy places he would go, and what may have seemed absurd to our guests that Thanksgiving was routine for us. We were determined that we were going to get that hundred dollars. Like most people though, we simply acted then thought rather than think then act – except Kelley.

Kelley searched along with everyone else, but mentally began to trace Papaw's steps in her mind. She remembered that he had gone out to feed the dogs and cats and checked to see if the dog had any extra teeth; you can't imagine how funny an old farm dog looks with a new set of uppers in his mouth. Then she remembered Papaw checking the mail, and looked in the mailbox to see if he had tried to send them parcel post. Step by step, Kelley slowly retraced his steps. The one important thing in retracing Papaw's steps was to not allow logic to intervene. Just because it doesn't seem logical for him to have put his teeth in the mailbox doesn't mean you should rule it out. Using this course of thinking, Kelley remembered that Papaw had been drinking a glass of iced tea earlier in the day.

Papaw drinking a plastic tumbler of ice tea during the day was common. He would take a few sips then put it back in the fridge for safe keeping. Then a few hours later, he would go back for another few sips. Kelley, not following a sense of logic, checked the fridge for one of Papaw's tumblers of tea, and found one. Then she looked in the glass and, voila, there were Papaw's teeth. Papaw was extremely appreciative, and Kelley had a "C" note for her efforts.

Teeth in tumblers, teeth on a wheel well, teeth in a burn barrel, or any other place was part of our life – it was normal and common, and the way we lived. The one place that you rarely found Papaw's teeth, however, was in his mouth. As odd as that sounds, it is the truth. The statement that you could almost always count on hearing from Mamaw was, "Philip, spit that tobacco out, put your teeth in, and get in here – church is about to begin."

The Golf Cart

Then the Spirit said to Philip, "Go over to this chariot and join it."

Acts 8:29

Papaw, until the day he died, served as the king over his estate as if he were the regent of a mighty kingdom. He knew every corner of his property, and every undulating contour of the land. The lush green land cascaded from the area where the house is to a creek that ribbons through the center of the property, then rises again on the far side of the stream butting up against his neighbors' properties. Every inch of that land he had covered many times, and knew it well.

In the early years that he owned the farm he walked every inch of fence line multiple times. As the years continued on he began to make the journey across the rolling countryside in either his pickup truck or on his tractor.

Falling trees and limbs, as well as not-so-well behaved cattle are pretty hard on fences and, as a result, the fence needs a lot of care and maintenance. Tree limbs were also pretty hard on the head when riding a tractor; they had a tendency to sneak up on you and thwack you in the face when you least expect it. For those reasons, and perhaps a strange obsession with tree limbs, Papaw incessantly picked up sticks, twigs, tree limbs, and any other form of wood that may have dared cross his path. He would pull dead ones out of trees, and pick up an endless supply of branches from the ground. This became such an obsession for him that it didn't even matter where he was, or whose property he was on; he still picked up sticks.

As he would stroll along he would pick up every stick that he came across. When I walked with him I was encouraged to do the same. Actually, encouraged is way too passive of a way of putting it; ordered or commanded comes a little closer. During his stroll across his farm land periodically there was a gully that had a tendency to wash out even further so that is where he would deposit this endless supply of twigs. From a very practical perspective it makes perfect sense; picking up one menace and using it to stop another menace. These same limbs also proved to be very useful in starting and keeping fires going in the various wood burning stoves and fire places. However, his single-minded focus on picking up twigs, sticks, branches and anything else that may come from a tree bordered on the obsessive compulsive side of things.

Anyone who knew Papaw at this point in his life would certainly have experienced this unique eccentricity of his; there was certainly much worse trouble that he could have gotten into. However, as he did get older his ability to make his rounds surveying his kingdom became more challenging because, as he would frequently share, "My knees are a sore as boils." The years of picking cotton and tobacco, and of hard work on the land had certainly taken a toll on him.

What really leveled the playing field for him was the year that his various children conspired and collaborated together, and purchased a golf cart for him from which he was able to survey his kingdom in style. In many ways that golf cart became his mistress over the next several years. He was able to go places and do things on it that I am positive it was never intended for. But, so were my litany of cousins.

The closest it came to being used for its intended purpose was when my cousins and I, along with our fathers and uncles would venture out into pasture as our makeshift golf driving range. We would start near the tractor shed and drive our golf balls well out into the pasture with the intention of going past the third telephone pole with our ball, and then returning to be the first to successfully hit the side of the tractor shed with our ball. I have not looked up the etymology of the phrase, "you couldn't hit the broadside of a barn with that thing," but I am in little doubt that it came from us unsuccessfully trying to hit that old tractor shed with our golf balls. It was embarrassing because it really is about 60 feet wide and about 15 feet tall – that is really a very broad side of a barn to miss – repeatedly, but we did. That old building was in very little danger from us coming anywhere close to it. Honestly, I think a big part of the joy for us was joy riding in the golf cart with reckless abandon to chase down and retrieve our balls.

To Papaw, however, this was a part of his farm machinery as much as his tractor, bailer, and any of his trailers. In the same way that Cesar would survey his empire from his chariot, this was Papaw's chariot and he was in no doubt the emperor of that land. He steered and powered that golf cart across hills and valleys that it was never intended for; perhaps that would explain Mamaw's reluctance to join him on these excursions to survey his land.

You see, she did appreciate the land and the joy it brought to the entire family. She too spent many hours walking over the land, and was often the one to bring in the family Christmas tree each year. However, she did not appreciate the fearless manner that Papaw would crest a hill and traverse a steep, mud covered incline that broke in multiple directions; especially when that same incline ended in a relative deep part of the creek that cuts through the property. Her recalcitrant ways when it came to joining him on his golf cart excursions were in no way an impediment to him navigating his own Wild West adventure, no matter how much she begged him not to.

One of the realities of golf carts is that they were never designed to be used in the manner that he did. Golf carts are designed to hold two relatively rotund men, their golf bags, and perhaps even a cooler containing some refreshing adult beverages. None of that was ever on Papaw's agenda for how to use his golf cart.

He would take it on very long adventures across his farm land, stopping every minute or so to pick up more sticks, limbs, and branches. The unfortunate soul who had decided it was a good idea to venture with him would become the Sherpa for him to pick up the various sticks that he pointed out, and it seemed that no matter how much his eyesight had waned in his later years he was still able to spot sticks to be picked up with hawkish attentiveness. The small ones were to be thrown into the gullies, but the larger ones he would keep for firewood. Inevitably, he would load the golf cart to the point his traveling companion was forced to walk. Of course, you would be expected to keep up beside him in the golf cart so that you could continue to retrieve the limbs he pointed out to you. If you stayed in the golf cart with him the weight of the amount of wood he was carrying on the incline, would drain the battery to the point that unless he kicked you out that both of you would have to walk, and he was certainly never going to be the one walking. So, enjoy your walk and your game of Pick Up Sticks.

Often, as I would visit their farm, I would be greeted with a quick hello, but just as quick, "You reckon you can have a look at that golf cart of mine; it's acting up something terrible." This, of course from his perspective, fit right into my profession and my degree in electrical engineering in much the same way that ceiling fans did.

Actually, I have always had a proclivity for electro-mechanical things. Mamaw and Papaw both recognized this and never missed an opportunity to capitalize on it. Once, Mamaw was concerned about her front porch light not going back out after a few minutes since it was on a motion sensor. She was right, I sat and watched it for about 15 minutes, and never did it go out. I looked at the sensor and it seemed to be setup correctly, so I just sat and watched and thought about it for a little while. Then, I went over and took the American flag down that was directly in front of it and brought it inside, and sat down again. After just a couple of minutes the light went out, and Mamaw exclaimed, "You fixed it!" She was quite amused when I pointed out to her what the problem was.

What Papaw presented to me in his golf cart's woes I took as a challenge, and was it ever a challenge. The wires, the switches, the motor, the batteries, etc. were all sourced and placed in the golf cart by the manufacturer who envisioned two rotund golfers and their small amount of equipment. They did not design it for an eighty-five-year-old man who weighed 150 pounds and 600 pounds of firewood, climbing a 45 degree, muddy incline. To say that the golf cart was in constant need of my attention is an extreme understatement.

Each time I would cut out a burned piece of wire and replace it, or resurface the contacts of the main switch – again – I would urge him to take it easy on it. He paid about as much attention to what I said as he would if I had invited him to go use the golf cart for its intended purpose of playing golf. By the way, he hated golf. I began to feel like the cardiologist who attempted to convince their patient who is at least twice their recommended body weight that the Golden Corral buffet is not quite what is meant by dieting. But how I kept that golf cart running for the balance of his life I will never know; it was on par with the oil and flour that never ran out for Elijah and the Widow of Zarephath. The miraculous survival of the golf cart is compounded in my mind as I remember my cousins enjoying it as well.

It is doubtful that I will ever forget the time I was at my grandparents' home doing something in the kitchen. From the kitchen window you have a very good vista of a significant amount of the farm. However, on this occasion, I did not need to see far at all. In fact, about 20 feet was more than sufficient as I watched no less than about 8 cousins and / or friends all on the golf cart at once and bounding across the yard with glee and joy. I had heard them long before I saw them as they boisterously made their way up the hill from the barn and across the yard, and then repeated it multiple times. I grabbed my tools, and prepared to repair that beloved golf cart one more time as this time it more closely resembled a clown car than a golf cart; it had many incarnations.

Ruby's Job

Likewise the Spirit helps us in our weakness; for we do not know how to pray as we ought, but that very Spirit intercedes with sighs too deep for words. And God, who searches the heart, knows what is the mind of the Spirit, because the Spirit intercedes for the saints according to the will of God.

Romans 8:26-27

There are days and circumstances that words simply escape you; you just don't know quite what to say. We have all been there, and we have all experienced that from time to time. We also have those incredible and very free souls in our lives that leave us absolutely speechless. On those days we pray that the Spirit helps us in our weakness; for we just really do not know what to say.

My incredible bride and I met early in our freshman year at college. At first, we were very close friends, but really had no romantic interest in each other. That first Christmas break when we spent several weeks apart put our relationship in a whole new perspective, and helped us to appreciate our love for one another in a way that has grown ever since.

Even before that realization, however, we were spending incredible amounts of time with each other, and often visiting each other's friends and families. I had spent many evenings with her and her grandparents who also lived in Charlotte, where we went to school. I liked them; they reminded me of my own grandparents.

Numerous times her grandfather and I would sit in the living room and talk while Emma and her grandmother chatted in the kitchen. I can't really explain why, but he and I seemed to really connect with one another and just enjoyed spending time in each other's company. Unfortunately, that did not last as long as I would have liked.

When Emma left on Christmas break we had become close friends who genuinely enjoyed spending a lot time with each other. During the course of that break both of us began to recognize a significant vacuum in our lives that could only be filled with each other. As she was returning from England after that break I called her grandparents to offer to pick her up. I used the excuse of bad weather, which was true enough, but the real reason was how much I had missed her and wanted to see her as soon as possible. Fortunately, her grandparents readily agreed to me picking her up from the airport; our reunion was sweet and incredible.

Not long after Emma had returned from England her father also came to spend time with Emma and her grandparents; this was my first opportunity to meet the man that would one day be my father-in-law. We got along amazingly well, as I had with Emma's grandparents already. However, what seems like only days after Emma's dad arrived from England, her grandfather suddenly and unexpectedly died.

Emma's pain was palpable, and I was humbled that our relationship had grown to the point that she sought me out for comfort in her moment of grief. I too felt a sense of loss for the man that I was just getting to know well, and I longed to know even better. He had reminded me of so many in my own family. He was genuine and approachable. I felt from him and Emma's grandmother alike a sense of appreciation that I had become a part of their granddaughter's life. Now, I mourned the relationship that could have gone so much further, as we each bid fare well to Emma's grandfather.

It was several days following Emma's grandfather's death before a funeral was able to be conducted; one of the most important people to be there also had to come from England, Emma's sister, Lizzy. Additionally, other family came from all across North and South Carolina, and further to say goodbye to a dear man loved by so many.

When Emma's sister arrived from England, she and I were sent to pick up Lizzy from the airport; everyone else was heavily involved in the planning for her grandfather's funeral. Lizzy had just found out about her grandfather's death before she boarded an airplane to come to the US for the funeral. She had no real time to process what was happening, and when she arrived she was way beyond the definition of tired. She was not only physically exhausted, she was also emotionally exhausted.

Emma and I borrowed her grandfather's car to pick Lizzy up, a Dodge Omni, or "Om-ma-nee" as her grandfather had pronounced it several times for me. As soon as we left the airport to return to the house Lizzy assumed a fetal position of sleep in the back seat and continued to catch up on some much needed sleep. Unfortunately,

Charlotte traffic is not always the most hospitable and cooperative, and as usual we ran into some significant traffic on our return trip. At one point, a car suddenly and unexpectedly braked in front of my causing me to have to do the same; Lizzy quickly became one with the floorboard of the backseat of the Omni. She used a lot of language that probably should not find its way into these pages to help me understand exactly how little she thought of that happening; I endeavored to allow a wider berth for the balance of our journey back to the house.

During all that was going on, I was meeting an endless stream of people from Emma's family that she had rarely seen because she grew up outside the US. However, I was meeting them all for the first time. It was awkward and uncomfortable to be so intimately intertwined in a family, experiencing such an incredible amount of grief when I really only knew one person there, and I had only known her for less than six months. However, at the same time, it was incredibly gratifying to be so warmly welcomed by this family as they each universally recognized how much Emma and I meant to one another. It was such an affirmation on our growing love and relationship that when I was invited to ride with Emma to the funeral with her family. I eagerly agreed and joined them.

Emma's family, as I discovered in this time with her, grieves out loud. I do not mean the loud and mournful wailing that may accompany some families at a death; I mean instead the loud and boisterous laughter of a family who loves to be in each other's company.

Most funeral homes are somber and serene places where the vast majority of the people there are attempting to maintain a level of silence that would ensure the dead person stays asleep; this is not the case with Emma's family. If anything, it would seem that they are attempting to wake the dead.

All during the visitation at the funeral home it was interesting to note the look on the various funeral directors' faces. Emma's family was telling stories of all that had happened in their family over the years. They shared stories of their times at the home "in the country", times at the beach, times on various trips, and just about any other story you could think of. They especially wanted to bring me up to speed on what it meant to be part of this family. Each story was loud and boisterous as it seemed a competition existed in filling in the details, and the whole thing was accompanied by tremendous amounts of laughter. The funeral directors each seemed uncomfortable and anxious since all the other families using the funeral home that night were as quiet as church mice. For Emma's family, they kept making sure that the doors stayed closed to try to contain some of the hilarity. It was probably one of the most healing visitations that I have ever been to.

Following visitation, funeral, and burial I was invited to another of Emma's family traditions, going to the fish camp. Where I had grown up, going to the fish camp was next to going to church as far as sacred events; I was not going to miss this.

Fish camps are pretty much all constructed the same way. They have all sorts kitschy decorations around of all things nautical like ship's helms and compasses, various seagoing pictures, and often even wait staff dressed as pirates. The tables inevitably have a red and white checkered tablecloth over Formica tables. The chairs are standard wooden ladder back chairs, and all drinks are served in clear or red plastic tumblers. You don't even need to order it because hush puppies will be delivered to every table along with generous helpings of a butter-like substance. It is AWESOME, and this one did not let me down with tradition; it was all there.

As we gathered at the fish camp I met one of the most incredible people ever, Emma's great-aunt Ruby. Ruby was Emma's grandmother's older sister, and was probably one of the most uninhibited people that I have ever come across in my life; she was exactly what Emma's grandmother needed at that time to help her grieve her husband's death.

Throughout the evening Emma sat beside me, but Ruby was on the other side. The more beers that Ruby drank the more she flirted with me; that was a little odd. I suspect most people there thought I had a pretty bad sunburn because I was blushing the entire evening from her aunt's advances. On the other side of Ruby sat Emma's grandmother who went back and forth the entire evening between laughing at Ruby's antics and trying to rein her in some; that was a lost cause. Ruby was most definitely her own person and no one was ever going to rein her in.

Ruby was already a little over 70-years-old at this point and had been a widow herself for a number of years. However, she still actively worked. The one thing that Ruby wouldn't say though is what she did, but boy did she laugh about it.

Ruby talked about having a number of "free samples" from her employer, but never talked about who her employer was or what the product was. Everyone else, but me, seemed to know exactly where Ruby worked and what she did, but they were not saying a word. Ruby even offered at one point to empty out one of the hush puppy baskets and fill it with "free samples" and pass it around the table; Emma's grandmother all but begged her not to. I spent the balance of our meal trying to figure out the puzzle of this conversation, but I was able to discern nothing.

As we walked out of the fish camp after dinner Emma was on my arm and Ruby walked, rather unsteadily, nearby. Ruby came close, and slipped her hand in the hip pocket of my jeans, putting something in my pocket. As she did that did that she whispered in my ear, "Here Darlin', you might want this later on."

I didn't even look to see what she put in my pocket until we were long gone; I was still trying to process Emma's great-aunt basically groping my butt. Of all the things you may expect at a family gathering that is not typically on the list. What I found in my pocket, however, took it to a whole new level.

After we left the parking lot I finally pulled out what Ruby left in my pocket when Emma and I were alone in the car. Ruby had placed a premium, lamb skin condom in my pocket. How I maintained bladder control and did not crash the car at that moment is anyone's guess. What I came to learn was that Ruby had recently gotten a job at the local Trojan factory as a quality assurance inspector. Yep, basically this septuagenarian was a condom tester.

As odd of an occasion as this may seem, it was exactly what Emma, her grandmother, her sister, and all needed. They all laughed harder than they had in a long time. They all left that evening after watching Ruby interact with me and watching me try to figure out what on earth this woman was talking about with a significant weight lifted off them. Ruby was the comic relief and I was her foil. I was left, however, completely speechless, but deeply loved.

Sunday School With Sam

Honor your father and your mother, so that your days may be long in the land that
the Lord your God is giving you.

Exodus 20:12

As Granddaddy got up in years, his mind began to become cloudy. At first, it was almost imperceptible. He would simply forget where he put his keys, or the turn to make to go to the grocery store. He would typically recover quickly, and no one was any the wiser. Gradually, however, he got to the point where a normal 9-5 job was out of the question, but he was still a good worker and wanted to contribute. His church was kind enough to allow him to do some of the grounds maintenance. It was a small job, where he couldn't get into much trouble, but after time even that became impossible.

While he still could, he and my grandmother went to church every week. They sang in the choir, taught Sunday school, and participated in any number of ministries around their church. For some reason, they had almost always gone to separate adult classes; he to the men's and she to the women's. One Easter, my girlfriend (who is now my lovely wife) and I joined them for church. I went with him to his men's class, and she with my grandmother to her women's class. This really pleased my grandmother, because it had been a while since she was able to go to her own class for fear that my grandfather would get into some mischief or unknowingly wander off.

My grandfather and I walked into the class and greeted some of the members before we sat down. At this point, I couldn't really figure out what all the fuss was about my grandfather. He seemed perfectly normal to me. Maybe getting a little older, but still basically the same man I had known and loved for years. We sat down and prepared for the day's lesson. The class leader got up and said, "Sam, I see you have a guest with you here today," indicating towards me, "would you like to introduce him?"

My grandfather stood up with such enthusiasm and a big proud smile on his face. I just knew that he was going to lavish praises on me, and boast about how proud he was to have his grandson with him that day; he always had in the past. Then, he stood there and pointed to me and said, "Yes I would, I would like to introduce my longtime friend, Ralph Barnhart."

As hard as I racked my brain, I had no clue who Ralph was; it was not a name that I had ever heard. I couldn't believe it; my grandfather had no idea who I was. This was a punch in the gut that I was not prepared for, and it really hit me hard. As I later discovered, he had introduced me as someone he hadn't seen in about 30 years; long before I was even born.

I quickly interceded and smiled saying, "Granddaddy, you know I'm your grandson John David." He smiled, cut up a little and laughed about it. However, it really hit me then, that he was truly gone. His mind was going to be with the Lord much faster than his body was. When he died, a few years later, my family was both amused and comforted by the fact that my grandfather was finally reuniting with his mind.

He and I still loved talking shop together. For most of his professional career he was a plant engineer for various textile plants around the Carolinas, Virginia, and Texas. His knowledge of things technical always seemed a little dated to me, but accurate. I worked in the same field for quite a few years, and knew quite well what he was speaking of. My mother and my aunt always thought he was talking gibberish, but I assured them that he was dead on. Of course it was dead on for about 50 years ago, but it was still dead on. I could always get a feel for where he was in time based on the technology he was talking about. It was as if I had a private doorway into his psyche that no one else could see. I cherished that he and I could at least still share this secret language together long after no one else could communicate with him. Based on "when he was" I was able to guide my conversation with him so that, to him, it was present day. We would talk about the motor he was working on, the transformer he reconnected, or the generator set that was giving him a hard time.

One thing I never quite understood, and was a little spooked by, was the fact that he called me Ralph until the day that Ralph died. Then he just didn't know what to call me, so he didn't. We didn't realize this fact until some family had heard through the grapevine of Ralph's death. Granddadddy had no way of knowing at all, or even comprehending at that point that Ralph had died, but somehow I think his spirit knew.

It was sad to watch him go. It amazed me just how fast he went. It would come in spurts. For a year or more at a time, I would see no perceptible change in him. Then something would snap, and it would seem as if he were making up for lost time over about a two-month period. It was painful for all of us to watch. Each of us dealt with it in our own way. We were all drawn to him, and we all visited him.

The last months of his life I would often visit him in the assisted care facility that he was in, and eventually died in. During this time pretty much all meaningful conversation had stopped, and if you got a grunt you were lucky. Sitting, and reading passages of scripture to him, or talking with him about my day were meaningful to me beyond measure. He would still look at you and smile, and squeeze your hand when you held his reminding me of the days that he would try to show me his strength by the firmness of his grip. It was painful to see him go, but I felt a sense of peace about it in the way that he seemed to welcome death as an old friend. Perhaps now he and Ralph are laughing together again, fixing the Lord's textile mills.

Roles Reversed

Do not speak harshly to an older man, but speak to him as to a father, to younger men as brothers, to older women as mothers, to younger women as sisters – with absolute purity ... And whoever does not provide for relatives, and especially for family members, has denied the faith and is worse than an unbeliever.

1 Timothy 5:1, 8

The honor we have in serving our family is not repaid in gold or silver. Nor is it repaid in anything tangible, but it is repaid in God's blessings on us and our family members. It is far and away one of the most difficult ministries that we ever feel called into, to care for those who cared for us in our younger years. But, this is one of the most rewarding ministries in the way that we are allowed to serve those whom we love the most by giving the most we have to give – ourselves.

As each of my grandparents reached their final years their specific needs varied quite a bit. Some needed full-time, hands-on care. Others needed much less care until the very end. All needed something, and uniformly I was blown away by the way my entire family came together to provide that ministry. I was also humbled in the way that I felt God's presence and blessing in the small amount that I was able to provide, but it was some of the most meaningful ministry that I have ever enjoyed.

As my grandparents entered their twilight years, it became necessary for some of them to go into nursing homes. Others, we were able to care for at home. My mother's father, Granddaddy, was the first to need the skilled nursing care found only in a nursing home. This happened shortly after I got out of the Navy and started college. His first nursing home was just 15 minutes from where I was going to school at the time, so I was able to visit him relatively often. Each visit was an event in and of itself. Sometimes, I would just read to him. Other times, the entire family, along with local police, would be out trying to find where he ran off to this time. It was always an adventure.

The aging of grandparents is a very unique experience to go through. Although, it was very painful, it was also very rewarding. My grandparents each touched my life in very different ways as they led me through my early years. Then as I helped them through their final years, they each again led me in very different ways.

When you are young, just learning how to master life's most basic functions, and learning what a function is and why you care; your grandparents are inevitably there to help show you the way. Many of these times it will be to your parents' amusement. One of my grandfathers tried for years to get me to chew tobacco, calling it his "worm medicine." It must have worked, for as far as I know he never had worms.

My grandparents were there when I took my first steps. They were there again when I got my first stitches. They were there when I read my first words. They were there when I drew my first picture. They were there when I married my lovely wife. In the events of my life that mattered, they were there, and they loved and supported me. They were even there, all of them, when my parents could no longer see eye to eye and went their separate ways. I am one of those extremely fortunate people who had more grandparents alive when I graduated high school than most people ever know. When I graduated high school, I had two great-grandmothers, three grandfathers, and three grandmothers all living. Although my stepfather never officially adopted me, I always viewed him as my father as well as my biological father, just as he has always viewed me as his son. The same was true with his parents; they were just as much my grandparents as my biological grandparents.

During the years that I needed their assistance just to make it day to day, they would be there for me; and they thought nothing of it. Each of them took their turns at changing my diaper and feeding me. They held me close when I needed love, and they corrected me when I needed it. They opened the world to me and showed me how to appreciate and love God's creation.

As I grew older, they became my mentors. They told me funny stories about my parents growing up and about them growing up. They would go on for hours about how they cared for me when I was still a toddler, and how they loved it. It seemed that they missed changing my diaper and giving me a bath. We became friends for a while. They were self-sufficient and so was I. Unfortunately, this time was fleeting; the aging process stops for no one. The time they each spent with me as an adult and them with all their faculties was way too short, and I long for that time every day.

It wasn't long before their age caught up with them. One by one their bodies, and sometimes, their minds began to fail them. They were unable to take care of themselves. They could no longer bathe or dress themselves. They could not remember where they left their watch, and really didn't care. One by one they passed from this world and showed me how to die with the same dignity that they showed me how to live. As they each approached their final days, they each opened Heaven for me in slightly different ways. They approached their deaths with no more trepidation than you would expect for one of them going to dinner. They were tired, and they were ready to see God face to face in a way they had only dreamt of.

Granddaddy was the first to go; he developed Alzheimer's. Alzheimer's disease is a cruel disease that robs a person of who they are long before their body stops functioning optimally. Granddaddy's progression of this disease was silent and deceptive at first, but quickly got to the point where he did not remember any of us. For a while, it was not clear what was going on; he seemed normal, and was generally able to function. He began by making simple mistakes; not remembering why he went to the store. He couldn't remember which turn to make to get home, which keys fit the house, or any of the other basic day to day functions that allowed him to live normally. From there the disease progressed slowly, but relentlessly. For years he was able to continue working at the church and doing small craft jobs. He continued to tinker in his workshop and work in the yard. For a time I remember receiving letter after letter from my grandmother telling me how my grandfather was raking the leaves. The disease was so cruel that it did not even allow him to remember that he had just raked the leaves. Eventually, the cruel disease robbed him of the dignity of even knowing who my grandmother was.

Just as slowly as his disease caught up to him our family recognized it too. For a significant period of time each of us denied that there was even a problem. We were each convinced that our father / grandfather could not possibly be having this sort of problem. We desperately tried to deceive ourselves into believing that all of these "coincidences" were simple mistakes and tried to rationalize them away. That tactic worked for a while, but to the detriment of our family. By our denying that there was a much more significant issue and delaying getting my grandfather the more professional help that he desperately needed, we put him and my grandmother under undue stress and strain, and significant danger.

The aspect of the danger really hit us when a sheriff over an hour away from his home called to say that my grandfather was with him. For a reason known only to him, he drove away from the house and went to a town quite some distance from his home. Once there, Granddaddy wandered into the local school cafeteria and proceeded to eat lunch. To everyone else he was out of place, but to him he was right where he was supposed to be. Thank God the sheriff was a compassionate and patient man because he took the time to talk to my grandfather, and with compassion began to search for clues for who he was and why he was there.

The sheriff began to go through my grandfather's belongings after discovering that the information he could get from my grandfather directly was almost useless. In an effort to keep my grandfather from driving, my grandmother had taken his driver's license from him, but that did little to deter him from heading out. It is important to remember that when mental faculties are not at their fullest take the keys and not the license; they will not remember that you took the license or why they need a license to begin with. Unfortunately, all this made the sheriff's task of determining who this man was sitting in front of him much more challenging. Eventually, however, the sheriff found a business card for one of my grandfather's doctors in his wallet. Through the doctor's office, the sheriff was able to contact my grandmother and let her know the situation. Even more unfortunate was the fact that my grandfather had their only car.

My grandmother, extremely distraught, called my mother to help her out of this situation. My mother and my stepfather immediately got in the car to go meet the sheriff with my grandfather. When they arrived, my grandfather was still oblivious that anything was wrong, but was quite happy to see his daughter visit him "at work" in his mind, and was even happier that she had come to pick him up "from work". They picked him up, thanked the sheriff repeatedly, and took my grandfather home, but this time they did not let him keep the keys.

One of the more confusing aspects of talking with people who are suffering from some form of dementia, like Alzheimer's, is the fact that they seem to be in an entirely different space and time than everyone else. In my grandfather's case, he was somewhere in the late 50's or early 60's, at one of the factories in which he had worked. For my grandfather, during his more productive years, he was a plant engineer for a number of different textile factories around the Southeastern United States. Whenever he drifted off to another time or place in his mind, it was almost always at work in one of those factories.

As odd as it may seem, my grandfather's alternate place and time in his mind gave him and I a unique ability to communicate when others could no longer understand him. I could always discuss with him what he had been "working on" that day and how he had "fixed it". As an electrical engineer myself who worked in numerous textile mills, I understood the technology quite well. I also had repaired much of the same equipment in some of the same factories that he had once worked in. Based on what he was working on and the way he described it I could not only tell "where" he was, but "when" he was. These moments of semi-lucidity were precious to me, and I will treasure them forever. This was our special time with each other that oddly enough only seemed to confuse everyone else.

When my parents returned my grandfather home, after his little journey, the realization hit everyone very hard that things could not continue as they had. Life dealt us a cruel blow, and we had to face the fact that my grandfather needed professional assistance, around the clock, and only a skilled care facility could handle it. Within a few days the necessary arrangements were made and he was placed in a nursing home close to where I was going to school.

At first, as he had his moments of reasonable cognitive ability and I wondered why we had to subject him to being in a nursing home. Those moments, however, were few and far between and much more regular were his moments of complete and total confusion and dementia. As much as I did not like the idea of him being in a nursing home, I also recognized that no one person in our family could provide for him what he needed at that time. This was an extremely painful realization, but it is a step that every family has to go through, and each person in the family goes through this process differently.

Within about a year of my grandfather being placed in the nursing home, he completely wore out his welcome. In a period of just weeks he escaped with a good head of steam behind him, was caught numerous times in other residents' rooms who were female, had two women with similar mental capabilities to him get in a fight over him, and took another man's cane and hit him with it. The home basically expelled him, for lack of a better term. In case you don't know, when that happens, no facility will take the person and the state is forced to take custody of them. This was humbling for us all, and left us with no small amount of anxiety about what the future may look like.

The state taking custody of my grandfather was very traumatic to me. I had a hard enough time accepting the fact that he had to have some kind of care to begin with, but now he was becoming a "ward of the state." Looking back on it, I wish they would have taken custody of him years before. The local, privately owned, nursing home did not give my grandfather near the attention that the state institution was able to. In the years that he was at one of two different state institutions, he was better cared for than anywhere else he went. They gave him great one-on-one attention and they kept the family very well informed of his status, regularly. They didn't even get upset when he moved furniture around, one of his quirks that the nursing home got very upset about. Instead, and with minimal coaching, he ended up moving it right back, and was applauded for his much appreciated assistance in moving the furniture. It was definitely a more congenial and loving attitude that met him where he was rather than trying to fight against him.

It was at this point that conversation with him waned to almost nothing, and if there was conversation it was almost unintelligible. If we were lucky we could get just a few words out of him that made any sense at all, but usually we were not so fortunate.

Visiting him in one of these institutions was an adventure of epic proportion itself. The residents each have their own odd quirks about them, which give you just the smallest hint of the person they once were. Some were so compassionate that it was frightening, while others were so combative that it was frightening. The combative ones were usually watched very closely and the staff made it a point to know what triggers them to make sure that it did not occur.

The number of people that I have been in visiting one of these facilities would be a great case study for any psychologist looking at multiple personalities. I have been employers, employees, fathers, brothers, sons, and even on occasion, myself according to the person I was visiting or one of the other residents of the facility. My favorite, however, was when I was someone's son.

Once while visiting my grandfather in one of the state-run facilities he was in, my mother and I were sitting in the day room with him trying to get some conversation out of him. We mentioned various family members, no result. We mentioned church music, no result. We mentioned a problem with the tenter frame on the finishing floor, and we got a few grunts and a smile. By the way, a tenter frame is a textile machine used for making textiles a uniform width and not skewed. One thing we discovered with my grandfather very early on was that his work was his life, and conversations that entered into that realm usually elicited a response, if anything would.

While we were attempting to talk with my grandfather a lovely older lady approached me. She was wearing a nice looking flower print dress, bedroom slippers, and carrying a purse. I could tell by her intentional look that she was on a mission, but I could also tell by the bedroom slippers and the disheveled hair that her mission should be to stay safely in those corridors. Unfortunately, she did not agree with that sentiment and intended to make me part of her plan.

She curtly strode right up to me and said, "John!"

This obviously caught me a bit off guard. I thought that perhaps my previous estimation of who she was may have been a bit hasty; after all, she knew my name. I politely responded, "Yes ma'am."

"John Paul, you will take me home right this minute, I have my purse and I am ready to go."

"Well, uh, ma'am," stammering a bit as I groped for the right words, "I think you might have me confused with someone else. Perhaps it would be best if we sit down."

"No, I absolutely do not! I would know my own son anywhere. Now stop trying to confuse me and take me home! I brought you in this world and I will take you out!"

"Uh, oh, wow." From the eloquence of my response it is easy to see I was dumbfounded and my own mother was no help at this point. She was getting the giggle of her life watching me try to dance around this one. I have found that trying to rip them from whatever reality they exist in at that point is not all that helpful, so I tried to play along for a minute. "Mom, I don't think that it is quite time to go home yet. We are still visiting with Sam," as I indicated toward my own grandfather. "Perhaps, you would like to sit and talk with us."

Unfortunately, I found out how in charge this lady had been before her own dementia began to have its way with her, and there was to be no discussion about it, "I told you that I am ready to go now, and I meant it. Now get your coat and take me home."

Now my mom, not my new friend, became a big assistance in my quagmire, and she recommended to me, "Go get your coat, and take a long walk while you are at it." I did take her advice, and when I returned my pseudo-mother had abandoned me and had no idea of who I was again. Although the entire conversation was a bit tense and I was glad it was over it was a bit sad to come back and she did not remember me. Their minds are often so fragile and fleeting that we only get rare glimpses of the people who they once were.

When my grandfather was first institutionalized his body was still in fantastic condition. He had the mind of a child and the body of a fully grown, very powerful man. He was still very much an intimidating physical presence to any who encountered him, but he was, in reality, as gentle as a lamb. Gradually, his body began to be where his mind was, and little by little his body failed him. What made this truly difficult for us was when he had problems which required surgery; his mind never came back with him from the surgery.

This happened three or four times and each time what little cognitive ability he had dropped significantly. The first time was the most noticeable because after that he never even tried conversation any longer and his ability to walk on his own pretty much went with it.

We visited him in the hospital after that first surgery, and he barely acknowledged that we were there. We noticed that it had been several days since he had been shaved, and I took the initiative to try to shave him. I got some shave cream and a safety razor from the hospital staff and gently began to shave him. As I put the cream on his face I noticed a sense of relief and gratitude come across his wrinkled brow. He was a bit startled at first, but he somehow recognized me, and let me continue. When I took the razor and began to shave those coarse whiskers from his face he shaped his face to make it easier for me to do this task. He would lift his head a bit so that I could get under his chin and he poked his tongue in his cheek (no pun intended) to stretch the skin there to make it easier.

This was the first of many times that I had the opportunity to do something this intimate for one of my grandparents. It was a humbling, uplifting, and gut wrenching experience each and every time. I was humbled to be doing a task for them comparable to them serving me when I was just an infant and could not do for myself. I was humbled by the grace they showed, each of them, to allow me to do this task and even help me to do something so intimate with them. Some of them still had cognitive ability at this point and we would actually have a bit of conversation while I was serving them in this way. I was uplifted by this precious time that we were able to share as grandson and grandfather, or grandson and grandmother. At the same time, however, it was gut wrenching in that both they and I realized that their time on earth was quickly drawing to a close and there was nothing that either of us could do to prolong it. All we had left was the this awkward time that I was able to help them do the most basic of tasks that they could no longer do for themselves.

While I had the opportunity to serve each of my grandparents in some way like this, I was reminded of the account from John 13 where Jesus washes the disciples' feet. He humbled himself to be their servant, but, as Simon Peter found out, they had to humble themselves to allow him to serve them. In order for me to do these intimate tasks for my grandparents, each of us had to humble ourselves. I had to be humbled to be willing to shave them, put lotion on their arms and legs, help them use the restroom, or even change their diaper.

Doing these tasks is not for everyone, but if this opportunity arises no one should avoid them. If you need to cry, then cry, but share the moment. At the same time, don't be so somber that you take yourself so seriously that you forget to laugh; laugh and laugh heartily. This time together may be the most precious memories that you will carry with you of your loved ones for the rest of your life. Who knows, perhaps this same loved one may have carried with them this memory to the grave of doing the same for you when you were but an infant.

Granny's Birthday

Finally, brothers and sisters, farewell. Put things in order, listen to my appeal, agree
with one another, live in peace; and the God of love and peace will be with you.
Greet one another with a holy kiss. All the saints greet you. The grace of the
Lord Jesus Christ, the love of God, and the communion of the Holy Spirit be
with all of you.

2 Corinthians 13:11-13

There really is no easy way to say goodbye. Each of us along
life's journey, at different times and in different places, and for
different reasons will have to say goodbye. We may be bidding that
farewell to co-workers when we take a new job, we may be moving to
a new community, or we may be saying that final farewell that Paul
bids to those in Corinth.

For many people as our days on earth come to a close we know it
as well as everyone else does. Our bodies all will eventually wear out
and we will all surely die, but for people of faith this death is but a
passage to something much greater. We know, by faith, that this
death is only temporary and that we too will enjoy a resurrection like
Jesus did when our perishable bodies put on imperishability. Since,
by faith, we look forward to the resurrection of our bodies, we also
know that in order to be resurrected we must first die. Granny knew
this, and greeted death like a long lost friend. In many ways she not
only taught me how to live, but in this final act she taught me how to
die.

Granny was born April 1st, 1916, and was quite proud of the fact
that she was an "April Fool's" girl. Her birthday was always special
and always brought out the humor in the whole family. I had never
seen so many ways to poke fun at one day of the year, but we seemed
to take it to an art form. Granny's birthday that I remember the most,
however, was her last.

From my earliest memories I recall that Granny took birthdays
very seriously. Except for the years that I was enlisted in the Navy,
when no one could call me, Granny always called me early on the
morning of my birthday. Each year she would make the rounds of the
grandchildren and great-grandchildren, when they came, calling each

of us on our respective birthdays just to say how much she loved us and to remind us of how she first heard about each of our arrivals.

Like clockwork every year the phone would ring and a cheerful voice would greet me with, "Happy Birthday John David." No matter how groggy I was, this made me smile and made my day so much brighter. Granny would take just a couple of minutes retelling of the day I was born and how my father announced to her that I had arrived. Each year it was as if it was the first time she was experiencing this all over again. It was easy to tell that it was a joyful time for her too. She loved to celebrate a birthday and it seemed that brightening days was her mission in life. It was always a brief call, but it was always meaningful and heartfelt. And, never did I become too old for Granny's love or phone calls; today I miss them tremendously.

When possible, Granny would make an event of our birthdays. For much of my life we lived relatively close to her, which meant that I could expect to see a lot of her. Birthdays meant cakes, and balloons, and crafts, and games, and whatever else Granny could devise. The real beauty was that Granny took the time to get to know each of us, in a very personal way. For instance, I turned six just after the Apollo 11 mission of 1969 and my interest in being an astronaut peaked at that point; I was anxious to be the next Neil Armstrong or Buzz Aldrin. Granny wasted no time in picking up on this, and for my birthday I had a cake in the shape of a spaceship. My sister's was always a doll, or flowers, or Donny Osmond. No matter what it was, it was timely to what we were interested in at the time.

Granny's interest in continuing to know each of her grandchildren never waned. Even when her health began to fail, she would continue to take an interest in what was going on in our lives, and was never too busy to listen. She connected with us where we were without it feeling odd or out of place. Each grandchild also was quite interested in Granny's birthday. She always reminded us that she was born on April Fool's day and evidenced this in how much of a nut she was; not that she was as nutty as she claimed, but it made for a good story. Granny always found a way to cut up, even just a little on her birthday. Usually she would tell us goofy stories or play practical jokes on us, but was always full of laughter.

We loved our Granny with all our hearts and wanted nothing but the best life had to offer. One thing she had always wanted in life was to have an 80th birthday party, but no worse than we wanted to give her one. About 8 months before her 80th birthday the doctors unexpectedly found that she had a brain tumor.

The tumor showed itself by causing her to have headaches and some loss of balance. As a precaution, my aunt took her to the doctor who immediately ordered a series of test – only to confirm what had been feared. Within a couple of weeks of discovering the tumor surgery was performed in an effort to further confirm the nature of the tumor, and unfortunately the inoperability of it. I distinctly remember a sense of being overwhelmed by grief at this news, and as the doctor shared the news with us our family gathered in prayer, and prepared for the road ahead. Unfortunately, we had no idea then just how short that road was to be.

After Granny recovered from the surgery, she began a regimen of chemo and radiation treatments. For a while they seemed to be working. Granny's speech and balance improved, and she was even able to resume some of her artistic endeavors. Each of us was praising God for the renewed sense of hope we had for her. Then about three months into the treatments, she stopped responding to them. The tumor began to grow again, and once again we started to notice her speech and balance start to waver. For a short period of time she seemed to hold status quo, but even that was short lived.

Granny started to slowly fade, and each visit I had with her I noticed that she was a little less sure, a little more confused, and a little more tired. However, Granny still found so much pleasure in our visits and it obviously invigorated her to share this way. Gradually, she went from walking from room to room, to us wheeling her around in a wheelchair, to eventually being confined to her hospital bed provided by Hospice.

Granny's birthday was approaching as we began to make plans for her birthday party. In the back of our minds, although none of us wanted to say so out loud, each of us knew that this would most likely be her last birthday party. By actually saying this we feared that it would actually come true, so we kept it to ourselves. We blindly went on making our plans as if Granny would live forever. However, the closer we got the less likely it seemed that Granny would even make it to her birthday. So, thinking outside the box, moved her party up to the week before her birthday.

Granny's Birthday

On the day of the party, Granny was so tired and weak, and so elated for so many people that loved her to be coming by just to say how much they loved her. Each person that came would sit with Granny for just a few minutes and tell her happy birthday. They would each talk about how they appreciated her friendship and Granny would smile. She still had the faculties enough to squeeze a hand or attempt a feeble smile, but that was about all she could muster. As I got to spend my time with her, she held my hand and we smiled at each other. I told her about the things that were going on in my life, wished her a happy birthday, and told her that I loved her. She smiled and was able to mouth, "I love you," and "thank you."

Although her birthday was less than a week later, Granny didn't make it – here on earth. She ended up spending her 80th birthday in the arms of a loving God. However, the gift she gave us in love over the years, in making sure that each of us knew that we were special is enough to last several lifetimes.

Of all the deaths I have ever experienced in my life, hers I felt in a way that surprised me and others. The day that she breathed her last I had left work a few minutes early in order to spend a few more precious moments with my beloved grandmother. My wife taught school that year a little closer to where Granny was and went straight there after school; I was to meet her there.

When I was still about 20 minutes from being with her I suddenly felt a rush come over me that I still cannot explain. It felt like something or someone blowing past me, even while I drove. I knew in a way that I cannot explain that Granny had just died. Within a couple of minutes my wife called me to let me know that Granny was gone. I replied the only way that I could at that moment, "I know." It pretty much freaked both of us out, but was indicative of the incredible relationship that I enjoyed with an incredible grandmother.

I believe that we have a deep spiritual relationship with our grandparents that words simply cannot fully explain. Granny is but one example of how I felt with each of my grandparents. With her, I enjoyed a bond that goes beyond words, but not beyond my heart.

Sunrise Service

But on the first day of the week, at early dawn, they came to the tomb, taking the
spices that they had prepared. They found the stone rolled away from the tomb,
but when they went in, they did not find the body. While they were perplexed
about this, suddenly two men in dazzling clothes stood beside them. The
women were terrified and bowed their faces to the ground, but the men said to
them, "Why do you look for the living among the dead? He is not here, but has
risen. Remember how he told you, while he was still in Galilee, that the Son of
Man must be handed over to sinners, and be crucified, and on the third day rise
again." Then they remembered his words, and returning from the tomb, they
told all this to the eleven and to all the rest.

Luke 24:1-9

In the earliest days of the church, while the original Apostles
were still actively engaged in the leadership of this fledgling faith,
many of the celebrations in the church we enjoy today were not part
of its reality. There was no Christmas celebration. There was no
celebration of Epiphany. There was no celebration of Pentecost. The
seasons of Advent, Lent, and Pentecost were not woven into the fabric
of the church yet. But, Easter was.

Easter was celebrated every Sunday, as recognition of the day
that our Lord rose from the tomb. Every Sunday was, in a sense, a
mini celebration of Easter. This is why the majority of the Christian
community gathers for worship on Sunday to this day; each week we
celebrate resurrection.

This does not take away from the importance of Easter Day,
which we celebrate annually. Each year, in communities all around
the world, we gather in a myriad of venues, worship styles, and
languages to celebrate this holy and auspicious day, the day of
resurrection.

Mamaw loved going to church. Missing Sunday worship and
Sunday school to her was anathema; she just wasn't going to do it.
She loved gathering with her long-time friends to celebrate this mini
Easter every Sunday and to hear the words of promise, hope, and
salvation. She loved the prayers and she loved the music, and being
able to enjoy all this with her family was heaven on earth to her.
However, as with many people, as she aged and her body became

frailer this became more and more challenging, and ultimately impossible.

Mamaw, despite her frailty, fought on, and fought valiantly to maintain this deeply held value in her life. About a year before her death she adopted the practice of rising very early on Sunday mornings, eating a meager breakfast, bathing and dressing before returning to her bed to rest from the exertion those activities brought. Then, rested again, she rose, straightened her hair and headed to church. Immediately after church, she returned home to rest so that she had the energy to prepare lunch for herself. Despite all this effort and exhaustion, her soul was lifted and inwardly she rejoiced at having been able to participate in worship. A few months before her death, however, even this regimen proved to be too great, and she was no longer able to make it to church at all.

I knew how much this weighed on her, and the emotional and spiritual pain that not being able to gather with her church caused her. As a matter of fact, a number of us in the greater family noticed this, and it grieved each of us on her behalf.

At this point, it was about three months until Easter and I discussed with some of my family this concern, but I also had a possible solution. I recommended to them that we bring church to her. They were not quite sure what I meant, so I explained that Easter was coming soon and that the tradition of an Easter sunrise service is one that many churches enjoy. I proposed that we conduct an Easter sunrise service right there on the front yard, invite friends and family, and Mamaw would have to go no further than her own front porch to join us. I was excited when they told me that it was a great idea. I was terrified when they told me to go ahead and do it. Oh my gosh, what have I gotten myself into?!?

The next three months were a whirlwind of activity that changed my life forever. I began to plan the service and plot out in my head how it would all work. I also spoke with one of my cousins, James, about conducting a family golf tournament the same weekend. Both plans moved forward and took on a life of their own.

Having been a Scoutmaster for a number of years I was used to conducting worship services on the side of a trail on Sunday morning. Gathering a group of boys by a stream and talking about our faith and the wonder of God's creation around us was comfortable and easy.

Planning an Easter sunrise service, however, was way beyond anything I had ever done.

The closer we got to Easter that year it seemed the faster Mamaw's health declined. We all hoped and prayed that she would be able to last until that great day, but her body was simply too weak. About three weeks before Easter, surrounded by her family and friends, she breathed her last.

Within just a few days we were gathered in that small country Methodist church, bidding farewell to a beloved grandmother, friend, mother, and saintly Christian woman. In the midst of our tears, however, was joy because we knew, by faith, that this death was not the end, and that she was now reunited with her beloved Philip, and her parents, and a litany of others who held a part of her heart. So we cried, and we celebrated.

During the course of the time around her funeral, there was some discussion about whether or not to continue with the sunrise service. Ultimately, as an aspect of our continued family healing, we decided to gather as we had planned in celebration of all that our God had done.

I had mentioned to Mamaw's pastor during the preparation for her funeral that we had plans to conduct the Easter sunrise service at the house, and if any from the church wanted to join us that we would be honored to have them. Her pastor told me that they appreciated the offer, but the church already had plans in conjunction with another church in town. However, less than two weeks from Easter Mamaw's pastor called to say that their Easter sunrise plans had fallen through and wondered if they could join us. I told her that would be incredible, but we may need a few more chairs and an extra pot of coffee or two; all was provided.

As mentioned, not having prepared or conducted a worship service of this magnitude before I was a bit apprehensive, but determined. Advice is something that all should be comfortable seeking, so I sought out my pastor to help me review my plans and preparation. While I was at the church for a Scout meeting, I quickly stopped by his office, explained to him what was going on, and asked him to read over my planned order of service and sermon. I wasn't expecting too much; I just wanted to make sure that I wasn't throwing around too terribly much heresy – a little is OK.

Peter Setzer, my pastor, is a big man. He towers over me by nearly a foot, with enormous and loving hands. When he came and sought me out about half an hour later I wasn't quite prepared. I had been under the impression that we would simply talk later. When that enormous and loving man grabbed me by the lapels, pushed me into the wall and said, "Quit your job now and go to seminary now!" I nearly came out of my skin. Clearly this man has lost all connection with his ability to objectively reason and for clear thought. But, no, he was deadly serious and he scared me to death.

I stammered and stuttered, and eventually spit out, "I'm an engineer. I can't go to seminary." I couldn't begin to fathom how God could possibly use an engineer as a pastor; it's just ludicrous. I tried my best to explain to him that this was just a one-time thing, and that I had no intention of ever leaving the engineering profession; I simply enjoyed it way too much. He did back down, but not much. He offered some great advice about conducting the service and sent me on my way, but his words stuck with me.

The Saturday of Easter weekend, we gathered for our family golf tournament; it was fun beyond compare. We laughed and enjoyed our fellowship in a way that has us bonded to one another for many years to come. After the golf tournament we returned to the farmhouse and started setting up for Easter morning. We had gone to the church and gathered supplies for the next day, including about 80 chairs. We knew that about 30-40 would be there from just the family and just went crazy and got about 40 more in case others showed up.

Gathering my cousins for a choir was an activity that goes beyond my wildest dreams. I had visions of the Mormon Tabernacle Choir performing in incredible four-part harmony. What I got was the Mormon Tabernacle Baseball Team who thought harmony was hominy grits to be plied with butter, salt, and pepper. I aimed my sights a bit lower and was exceedingly pleased with the faithful and loving response my cousins who mean more to me than words can express. We sang with joy and enthusiasm, and had a great time doing it. The song we sang together, *Have You Seen Jesus My Lord*, became the centerpiece of the homily I shared that morning.

On Easter morning I arrived at the old farmhouse about an hour before sunrise. Chairs were in place. A large wooden cross had been erected and placed on the lawn, draped with a white stole and flowers.

Bulletins were prepared, and hot coffee was already on. It was quiet and serene; just peaceful and pleasant. No one beyond a few family members was there yet.

Just before time for the service to begin I walked out of the old farmhouse to see all 80 chairs filled and nearly 20 more people gathered around the fringes; I still don't know how I didn't weep like a baby at that moment. I looked upon the faces of friends and family who have each stolen a piece of my heart, and words can never fully express the love that I feel for each of them.

The morning was crisp and cool. Many were bundled up in warm jackets, and even a few had commandeered a blanket from one of the beds and wrapped it around themselves. The early glow of the sunrise was starting to light up the day, and we all gazed upon the misty pasture spreading out beside the house in wondrous awe. That day, we all stood on holy ground.

Leading my family and friends in worship that day felt right in a way that nothing else ever had. I was wrapped in a warm embrace of love by God and my family in a way that blessed me beyond compare. However, I was still not ready to leave my job as an engineer.

After worship the crowd gathered around tables we had already set up for breakfast. We sat and talked and continued to share the memories of our family and our faith for some time to come. During breakfast, Mamaw's pastor sat with me for a while and echoed the sentiments of my own pastor; although in not quite so forceful of a manner. Over a cup of coffee and some homemade biscuits, she listened to all my reasons "why not" and offered a few "why I should" that I could not ignore, but I did for the moment.

The whole next year I reflected on the experience of leading that Easter service; it changed me irreparably. We gathered again for the next three years doing the same, but the next year was pivotal for me.

The planning, the golf tournament, and everything moved along much as that first Easter sunrise service had. But, God worked on me in an unexpected way throughout that year. As much as I tried to sluff off a sense of call to ministry I could not. Finally, just days after Easter that second year, I took my incredible wife to dinner for her birthday.

As she and I enjoyed our dinner and relished each other's company I shared with her the feeling that I had about what our pastor had said, about what Mamaw's pastor had said, and the experience of leading that service. I explained to her that as much as I want to ignore this that I no longer feel like I can, and I need to take it more seriously. Bottom line, I believe I need to explore going to seminary. But, I also want to explore going back in the Navy as a chaplain.

Her response to me was more confirmation than just about anything I could have ever asked for. She explained that she had known for years that this day would come, and she was planning for it. She said that over the previous several years that she had been doing different things with our family finances to put us in a better position for this day, and that she was ready to take that leap of faith with me.

Now, one bit of truth in this situation was that when I finally told her that I planned to explore this whole thing more and consider going to seminary her heart did momentarily stop. He thoughts went to, "Oh my God. I'm going to be a pastor's wife." She really did not like that idea at all. Then, when I mentioned that I would also be exploring going back in the Navy as a chaplain she breathed a sigh of relief, "Oh, good. I can be an officer's wife; that's much better."

Within a few months all of my essays were written and my applications were sent off. It was scary, but the right move for me to make.

As I reflect back on this entire episode in my life I can't help but notice how life came from death. In many ways, it was my grandmother's death, or her approaching death, that motivated me to move forward in this unique calling I have found myself in. Her death was painful, but I doubt that I would have made the same decisions had that tragedy not occurred in our family. I doubt that I would have gone down this path had I not enjoyed the loving relationship that I have with my family. This family, filled with so much faith, hope, and love has propelled me into places I would never have dreamed of.

Just over two years following Mamaw's death I left my career as an engineer and found myself sitting in a classroom in seminary. In many ways I was still in denial that this could ever work, but in an effort to humor God and others I would at least give it a try. But, make no mistake about it; I do still keep my toolbox around just in case this whole chaplain thing doesn't work out.

The Golf Tournament

Then our mouth was filled with laughter, and our tongue with shouts of joy; then it was said among the nations, "The Lord has done great things for them." The Lord has done great things for us, and we rejoiced.

Psalm 126:2-3

The golf tournament that arose as part of our Easter weekend festivities became a thing of legend itself. Friends and family gathered from near and far. There were some that played golf on a regular basis with some significant level of skill and there were some who had heard of the game, but had yet to pick up a golf club before. No matter the skill, the objective was to have fun, and the objective was thoroughly met.

For several years that I was able to participate a good friend of mine, Drew, was able to join us in the festivities. His introduction to our family was astounding. Even more astounding was the fact that he kept coming back after his initial experiences with us.

The first year that Drew gathered with us he and I met with a number of family members at the old farmhouse for yet another cup of coffee and a sausage biscuit; you really can't have too much of either. In the midst of enjoying our biscuit and coffee, however, a crisis erupted - the kitchen sink was no longer draining properly.

In homes built with indoor plumbing from the outset the approach to such a crisis simple. You open the trap or the clean-out and, well, you clean it out. For a sink that was there before the house had indoor plumbing and was never plumbed to the septic system, the process becomes slightly more complex. We had to trace the drain line to where it terminated down near the barn and clear away the debris from the end of the line.

Wearing our golf jerseys and armed with plenty of enthusiasm we charged off en masse to the barn in search of the recalcitrant drain to correct its evil ways. Shovel, rakes, hoes, and a wide variety of implements of destruction were picked up and hoisted into the air as we made our way to the barn. Honestly, we looked like a poorly dressed mob seeking to destroy Frankenstein's monster; all that was missing was our torches.

Someone in the crowd then proclaimed they knew exactly where the drain terminated. With a crazed enthusiasm several attacked the suspected spot, creating a crater in the earth only to discover dirt and cow manure, but no drain.

"No, no, dig over here; this is the spot," was proclaimed by another with a sense of authority.

Like the frenzied crowd we had become we moved our operations a few feet to the right and began to rip away the soil once again to find the drain. No luck. No joy. But, we did have another hole several feet wide and several feet deep.

"Wait, this is it; I just know it is. Dig right here," indicating yet another spot, a little closer to the house.

We did not lose faith or even falter in their confidence. No, sir. We dug with even more enthusiasm because we knew that we were closing in on the elusive pipe. Another hole and gaping crater was uncovered, and still no drain.

As all of this excitement continues for another three or four holes, Drew watched in wrapped excitement. Actually, he was barely containing his laughter. Well, in truth, he wasn't containing his laughter at all as he told me, "Man, you Connollys sure know how to have a good time. Nobody digs a hole quite like you guys."

Eventually, my father, who owns a plumbing wholesale company, pulled out one of his fancy gadgets that is made for just exactly this circumstance. It was an expandable bulb that is placed on the end of a garden hose and then inserted into a clogged pipe to effectively blast out stubborn clogs with ease. Shortly after he did this a geyser erupted in the yard, but nowhere close to where we had a series of holes dug in the ground near the barn.

When this fountain of water emitted from the ground my uncle then remembered, "Oh yeah, we moved that about ten years ago when this clogged up the last time. That's where we put it alright."

A chorus of laughter filled the air. We all acknowledged that perhaps working smart and not hard should be a model we follow in the future. That morning, however, our model was working hard and not smart.

As we made our way to the golf course Drew continued to be nearly moved to tears of laughter by the antics of our family. "You guys are a riot."

"We are not always this way," I assured him. But, in contrition I must confess, I may have accidentally lied; sometimes we are worse.

We played in foursomes and had about 10 foursomes starting that day; it was great. As each team teed up we watched, and cajoled each other as we began. It was obvious that Tiger Woods place in the annals of golf history and legend was in no way threatened by us.

Our foursome was Drew, my sister, Karen, her husband, Scott, and me. We played "best ball" which means that for each stroke we take the best ball hit, and then all four of us hit our ball from there. The next shot we do that all over again. As if that were not making it easy enough we were also reasonably generous with our mulligans. I think I used all of mine just getting off the first tee to everyone's amusement; except, of course the golfers on the courses to our left and right. But, our fairway was completely clear from being threatened by my swings.

When we got to the third or fourth hole we were debating on whether we should play Karen's ball or Drew's. When Karen reached down to move some debris from around her ball Drew noticed that her thumbnail was painted black, but also spread across much of her thumb. Drew found this unusual and asked her about her unusual manicure.

Karen never missed a beat nor gave it a second thought, "I was painting my nipples."

It was some time, and after some significant cajoling by neighboring golfers to quiet down that Drew was able to rein in his laughter. He had assumed many things that could have resulted in her thumb being painted black, but never in his wildest of dreams was that on the list.

"No, no, it's not that you dirty boy! Where is your mind? Oh my gosh, get your head out of the gutter," Karen interjected. "I was painting nipples at work."

Laughter spewed forth once more. "What kind of work do you do that you would be painting anyone's nipples?"

Karen was exasperated, and none of us were helping very much at all with our own laughter. "Oh my goodness Drew. It's not that kind of nipple; it's a short piece of pipe that is threaded on both ends. I work for my father in the plumbing business."

"Really?" Drew was absolutely incredulous.

"Yes really. They were rusting and I needed to paint them for a customer." Karen tried to regain composure, because we actually needed to still decide which ball to hit and who was going to hit first. Obviously, none of us had enough composure to hit anything for the next several minutes.

When Drew and I were driving home later that day he was telling me how he never dreamed that so much could happen with plumbing in one day that could be so interesting. "But man, your family is crazy. Really funny, but crazy. We have to do this again."

Things Begin To Change

What then are we to say? Should we continue in sin in order that grace may
abound? By no means! How can we who died to sin go on living in it? Do you
not know that all of us who have been baptized into Christ Jesus were baptized
into his death? Therefore we have been buried with him by baptism into death,
so that, just as Christ was raised from the dead by the glory of the Father, so we
too might walk in newness of life. For if we have been united with him in a
death like his, we will certainly be united with him in a resurrection like his.
We know that our old self was crucified with him so that the body of sin might
be destroyed, and we might no longer be enslaved to sin. For whoever has died
is freed from sin. But if we have died with Christ, we believe that we will also
live with him. We know that Christ, being raised from the dead, will never die
again; death no longer has dominion over him. The death he died, he died to
sin, once for all; but the life he lives, he lives to God.

Romans 6:1-10

The years can truly creep up on you, and you never realize the
age that is beginning to show on your grandparents. What used to be
taken for granted now requires assistance. What used to be a private
act now becomes a public production. That transition for Mamaw and
Papaw came suddenly, and unexpectedly. It caught us all off guard,
and we scrambled to give them the assistance that they needed.

It had really only been a couple of years since my grandmother's
mother had died at the tender young age of 99. She had lived a long
and wonderful life as a mother, a schoolteacher, a grandmother, a
great-grandmother, and a great-great-grandmother. When her years
caught up with her, she moved in with her daughter – my
grandmother. With tender compassion and joy, my grandmother
cared for her aging mother with love and gentleness until the burden
became too heavy to carry. She then continued to care for her at a
nearby assisted care facility until my great-grandmother's death.

When Mamaw's mother died Mamaw still seemed young to us.
She was exhausted by the service she had rendered for the last several
years, but she seemed to still have a lot of life left in her, and a lot of
care yet to give. Papaw's age seemed to be catching up with him, but
even at that he still seemed to be full of energy. Papaw and Mamaw

both loved life, and lived it to its fullest. At the center of that life was God, family, and church.

Granny and Granddaddy's story is very much the same. For the last few years of Granny's mother's life, Granny and Granddaddy lived across the street from her, and were able to care for most of her needs. But that care seemed to take a significant toll on the caregivers.

I'm a rarity in that growing up I knew and knew well three sets of grandparents and two sets of great-grandparents. Each of these five sets of grandparents had a profound influence on me and my life, and yet they could not have been more different from each other.

Pawpaw Harrison, my mother's grandfather, was an engineer, a jokester, and a Texan. With an engineering background myself, I am in awe as I consider the various developments from an engineering perspective that he was either involved in or witness to. He once came home and announced to my grandmother, "Well, Bob, we burned a turkey today." My grandmother was Barbara, but he always called her Bob. What he was referring to though was the fact that he had been able to mess around with an early version of a microwave, and burned a turkey in the process.

As a jokester he was constantly pulling one stunt or another, and even his explanations of his faux pas in his later years were in the form of hilarity. At one point I noted that he had a bruise on his head, and I asked him where it came from. "Well, you see, I was bending down to get some toilet water on and the seat fell." In actuality he had just run into a shelf, but the story he shared was much more entertaining. Although he never served in the Navy he would have done well there. Sea stories are an important part of being in the Navy, and we don't let the truth interfere with a good sea story.

There were, of course, occasions where no embellishment was required. One night as he lay dreamily sleeping through the night, he dreamed that robbers were trying to threaten him and my great-grandmother. As the valiant eighty-year-old gentleman that he was he rose to his full stature as knight in shining armor and successfully fended them off. Of course, my great-grandmother awoke in the morning with a rather splendid shiner to show for his valiant efforts.

Although the Texan moved out of Texas and made a home in South Carolina for the last 40 years of his life, the Texan in him never died. He was immensely proud of his Texas heritage, and many of his eccentricities were as big as Texas. Combining the jokester and the Texan he once asked for a cup of coffee at a local restaurant where we were having dinner. The waitress obliged him with a fresh, hot cup of coffee set right in front of him. No sooner had she set the cup down and begun to walk away did he stop her, "Darlin'. Excuse me, Darlin'. You need to take this cup back and bring me another; I simply cannot drink this cup of coffee."

The young waitress looked at him absolutely crestfallen. She could not begin to imagine what could possibly be wrong with his cup of coffee; he hadn't even tasted it yet. "What's wrong with it sir?"

"Well, you see," he began, "this here cup is a right handed cup, and well, I'm left handed. I'm gonna' have to ask you to bring me a left handed cup."

"Excuse me?" The poor waitress was beside herself in confusion. She had never known that cups came in right hand and left hand versions.

"That's right, I need a left handed cup," he firmly announced.

"Well, OK sir. I'll see what I can do," she replied as she picked up his right handed cup and returned to the kitchen.

My grandmother, his daughter, simply looked at him and said, "Daddy, what on earth are you doin' to that poor girl? That's just not right."

I watched the whole scene not quite sure of what was going on and noted our waitress returning to our table. She was carrying what looked like to me the exact same cup of coffee. She quietly and efficiently sat his cup and saucer back on the table, exactly as it had been before, and then she paused. She stopped, looked him square in the eye and the placed her index finger on the handle of his cup of coffee and rotated it 180 degrees so that the handle was now facing to his left. Then, ever so quietly, stood back up. "Will this cup do sir?"

He gave her a big Cheshire cat smile and said, "That'll do just perfectly darlin'. Thank you very much." That night, our waitress went home with a Texas size tip of $50 from a jokester of an engineer from Texas.

His lovely bride, my Mawmaw Harrison, was a force to be reckoned with, and as delicate as a rose simultaneously. During WWII she went down to enlist in the Army along with one of her daughters, my aunt. By the time the day was over Mawmaw was in the Army and my aunt was not because she was not accepted; her health was not good enough for Army standards. The truly amazing thing about Mawmaw was at the point she entered the Army she was already a grandmother, north of 50 years old.

Mawmaw was initially sent to Charleston, SC as a place to put her and assigned to the enlisted club serving drinks. The irony was that she was a teetotaler, and didn't drink a drop of alcohol. This did not sit very well with her at all, and before long she was reassigned to Alaska.

She and a number of other ladies were assigned there together, mostly doing some variation of administrative tasks. Mawmaw was quite literally old enough to be the mother of pretty much every lady there, so they all affectionately called her, "Mom." In Alaska they soon discovered that she knew how to play the piano and the organ and was quickly reassigned to be a chaplain's assistant for the balance of her time in the Army. This made her extremely happy, but when the Army offered for anyone over the age of 50 an early discharge she was the first to raise her hand; she had already experienced as much fun as she could stand. During the time she was in Alaska, however, she was able to reunite with her son, my uncle, who had already been serving on active duty in the Navy for a number of years and was already the rank of Chief Petty Officer during that visit. Most of the soldiers assumed that he was an officer and kept saluting him, not realizing that he was a non-commissioned officer and did not rate a salute. Eventually, he tired of correcting the soldiers and just started returning their salutes with an equally crisp Navy salute.

Mawmaw's delicate side was as equally incredible and it relates to the skills she put to good use on behalf of the Army, she was a musician. Actually, she wasn't just any musician, she was an incredible musician. In the years following the War she was a very active member of the American Guild of Organists, and eventually would serve as the National President of that austere organization; not the kind of title they just pass out for fun.

Mawmaw's mixture of strength and beauty somewhat escaped me, however, at the tender age of 4. About the time I was born she crossed the threshold of her 70th year, and as most people are aware, few bodies are quite as lean in your 70's as they may have been in your 20's or 30's. Also, an inescapable truth is that children are not always known for their decorum. So, when I noticed that Mawmaw was not quite as slender as my mother or even her mother, Granny, I was foolish enough to comment on that fact, "Mawmaw is fat."

The gasps that ensued from my bluntness drew a rather significant vacuum on the room. Granny, very quickly, pulled me aside and pointed out that it is not polite to refer to someone as fat. This was a shocker to me. "But she is," I replied.

"She most certainly is not," Granny imparted, "she is pleasedly plump." Well, how do you argue with that? I have no idea of why that conversation has stuck with me all these years, but boy has it.

Grandpa Lackey, my father's maternal grandfather, could not have been more different from Pawpaw Harrison if you paid him. Both were tall; very tall in fact, and slender. Pawpaw had spent his life in academics and engineering, and Grandpa was a simple country farmer. Neither, however, thought he was better or worse than the other; they were just where they wanted to be doing what they wanted to do.

When people today tell me that they are building a new home for themselves I know that it is more euphemistic than reality. At most, people today may put on a coat of paint, but even that is often a stretch. When I say that Grandpa Lackey built his house that is exactly what I mean. The home he built, that my grandmother was born in, was rustic to the maximum degree. The foundation was large smooth stones that he gathered from the river and placed in just the right combination to level the old wooden floor as the home's foundation. With his hammer, his saw, his nails, his blood, his sweat, and his tears he assembled that humble house into a home that they would enjoy for years. It wasn't much to look at. It was not painted. The roof was tin but quite rusty. All the floorboards were in and in place, but you could clearly see the ground below through the small gaps between those floorboards. It was humble, but it got his family going.

As the years progressed he built another home not 50 feet from the first. This second home was more refined with a brick foundation and a large front porch from which he was able to survey the land rolling out in front of his house. Bedrooms, kitchen, dining room, and all were immaculately built and beautiful. This home too, he built with his own hands.

He did not stop with those, however. He dug a well and plumbed the water to his second home. He built a spectacular barn, and a storage building. He built a tobacco shed for drying the tobacco he raised. All the while, he raised the tobacco that provided his family's income, and he grew a garden and raised cows that kept his family fed.

In later years, after he had retired from the farming that had kept his family fed and housed for so many years, he would continue to make his way around his farm. He would often walk down the hill, behind the original home built, to the well house that he also built just to get a sip of water. This, of course, caused my great-grandmother, Grandma Lackey, much anxiety because his steadiness on his feet was not quite what had once been. But, also, a fear she once shared with me was that she was afraid the crawdads in the stream that ran under the well house would come through the spigot and get him in the mouth.

I was amused with her fear, but reminded through it of her love for my grandfather. She had always been one who was concerned for the welfare of others, especially in her chosen career of teaching. Grandma Lackey had taught at the local elementary school her entire adult life, and even years after she had retired it was easy to see the love she still had for the great calling of being a teacher. Whenever another family member, who was also a teacher, would talk with her about teaching her face would absolutely light up with joy. It was a beautiful thing to behold.

As each of these incredible grandparents faded from my life my life changed. My innocence faded as I had to come to grips with the reality of death and I had to experience firsthand the reality of the pain of death. With each of them, however, I began to see death in a different way.

Death is as much a part of life as birth is; you really will not have one without the other. But, from a faith perspective as a Christian, I have come to know that death is no more than a boundary that we must pass through in order to experience life in a whole new way. The Apostle Paul proclaims this so well, "Do you not know that all of us who have been baptized into Christ Jesus were baptized into his death? Therefore we have been buried with him by baptism into death, so that, just as Christ was raised from the dead by the glory of the Father, so we too might walk in newness of life." (Romans 6:3-4)

Until we die we cannot enjoy the resurrection that awaits us, and neither can those we love. Appropriately, we mourn the deaths of those whom we love, just as Jesus himself wept at the tomb of his friend Lazarus (John 11:35). Yet, we rejoice in the new life that those we love who have already died enjoy, as we ourselves know awaits us as well.

To capture all the stories of my grandparents would take several lifetimes, but these are an offering in love of what they gave me in love. These stories come to an end, but a resurrection of tears and laughter will follow as we share these and other stories together.

Epilogue

Now Jesus did many other signs in the presence of his disciples, which are not
written in this book. But these are written so that you may come to believe that
Jesus is the Messiah, the Son of God, and that through believing you may have
life in his name.

John 20:30-31

The gospel writer who penned the Gospel of John apparently knew so much more that could have been shared about Jesus, his ministry, and his life. However, he felt like he had accomplished an appropriate sampling to give a complete and accurate picture of all that Jesus was about so that belief would be fostered. I have pretty much reached the same conclusion with respect to the stories about my family.

The image that I have in my mind of each of my grandparents, and those that assumed that role in my life, is one of tremendous love and care. Each of them helped make me who I am, and each of them continue to be part of what it means to be my daughter and the generations that will follow her.

I have no doubt that these stories will raise the memories of other stories in myself and family members who enjoy these stories with me. These are OUR stories. These are the legacy that we pass to our children, grandchildren, and countless generations to follow. Our stories are healing. Our stories are our heritage. Our stories will give our children's therapists material to work with to help them recover.

I offer these stories contained here to my family. You are more precious to me than any of the words contained here will ever convey. But, these are offered that you may come to believe in the incredible family that we have.

Family Photos

Philip Connolly & Mr. Jim Cornelius (ca 1975)
Philip & Lucille Connolly (ca 1996)

See: Cider with Mr. Jim

Moving The Outhouse

Cider with Mr. Jim

Work on the Farm

Milking Time

Biltmore

Cheer for your team

The Golf Cart

A Grandfather's Blessing

Tobacco Road

Gospel Music

The Penhooker

Corn On The Cob

The Penhooker

Papaw's Teeth

Sunrise Service

Marion Aldon and Maggie Connolly (ca 2006)
See: Marion's Teeth

Madelyn Strawn (ca 2000)
John & Maggie Connolly and Lizzy Strawn (ca 2013)
See: Ruby's Job
Rook

John & Bob Connolly (ca 2006 at a wedding)

James & Tammy Connolly (ca 1996)
and Kelley Connolly (ca 2015)
See: Wedding Weekend
Papaw's Teeth

John Connolly & Karen Reighter (ca 1970)
See: The Golf Tournament

Jon & Linda Schmidt and Maggie Connolly (ca 2007)
See: A Bucket of Oil
Chute-a-par
Freshly Ironed Clothes

John Connolly, Winnie Harrison, & Karen Reighter (ca 1966)
and Julius Ceasar "JC" Harrison (ca 1965)
See: Coffee Cake
Spirits Are Ya There?
Things Begin To Change

John Connolly with Barbara Hiser
and Sam Hiser (ca 1964)
See: Doorknob For A Toy

Chute-a-par   Doughboy
Freshly Ironed Clothes   Picking a good climbing tree
A Hammer and a Four-Year-Old
Sunday School With Sam   Roles Reversed
Granny's Birthday   Things Begin To Change

Martha & Norman Schmidt (ca 1984)
See: A Balanced Meal
A Grandfather's Blessing

About the Author and Editor

John & Maggie Connolly (ca 2010)

John Connolly was born in Iredell County, NC, where many of these stories find their origin. He grew up, through his school-age years in Gaston County, NC and shortly after high school enlisted in the US Navy.

Following six years in the Navy, John returned to NC to go to college and pursue a career as an engineer, which he did. However, he also met one of the most influential people in his life, ever, in his wife, Emma while attending UNC Charlotte. From the time they met, they were inseparable. Although his family had always meant the world to John, meeting Emma only increased the love and joy he found in his family that also had grown to include her family.

After working as an engineer for 15 years and with Emma's encouragement, John left his career and stability as an engineer to go to seminary in preparation for ordination as a Lutheran pastor and eventual return to the Navy as a chaplain. In 2006 he returned to the Navy as a chaplain where he has served since.

Seminary was a tremendous time for both John and Emma, and no change could have been more significant than the introduction to the family of a daughter. Maggie entered their lives only days after Hurricane Ivan rolled through Pensacola, FL, where John was serving a local congregation.

Maggie, now in high school, truly was a tremendous help in editing and supporting this project. Of course, she had to fit this project in to her demanding schedule of her swim team, synchronized swim team, and a very demanding International Baccalaureate high school curriculum.

Her current ambitions are to complete high school and pursue a degree in journalism, but for now, she is thoroughly enjoying a rewarding life in high school. The future is bright and exciting as she writes the next chapters of our lives.

www.ingramcontent.com/pod-product-compliance
Lightning Source LLC
Chambersburg PA
CBHW031547040426
42452CB00006B/224